0p.15   19x14(07)

W9-BQK-895

The
Still Point
Dhammapada

ALSO BY GERI LARKIN

Stumbling Toward Enlightenment
Building a Business the Buddhist Way
Tap Dancing in Zen
First You Shave Your Head
Love Dharma

The Still Point Dhammapada

Living the Buddha's Essential Teachings

A Contemporary Rendering and Stories

Geri Larkin

HarperSanFrancisco
A Division of HarperCollins*Publishers*

AURORA PUBLIC LIBRARY

THE STILL POINT DHAMMAPADA: LIVING THE BUDDHA'S ESSENTIAL TEACHINGS. Copyright © 2003 by Still Point Zen Buddhist Temple. All rights reserved. Printed in the United States of America. No part of this book may be used or reproduced in any manner whatsoever without written permission except in the case of brief quotations embodied in critical articles and reviews. For information address Harper-Collins Publishers, Inc., 10 East 53rd Street, New York, NY 10022.

HarperCollins books may be purchased for educational, business, or sales promotional use. For information please write: Special Markets Department, Harper-Collins Publishers, Inc., 10 East 53rd Street, New York, NY 10022.

HarperCollins Web site: http://www.harpercollins.com
HarperCollins®, ☰®, and HarperSanFrancisco™ are
trademarks of HarperCollins Publishers, Inc.

FIRST EDITION
Designed by Joseph Rutt

Library of Congress Cataloging-in-Publication Data
Larkin, Geraldine A.
The still point Dhammapada : living the Buddha's essential teachings /
Geri Larkin. — 1st ed.
p. cm.
ISBN 0–06–051370–5 (cloth)
1. Tipiòaka. Suttapiòaka. Khuddakanikâya. Dhammapada—Commentaries.
I. Title.
BQ1377.L37 2003
294.3'82322—dc21   2002038734

03 04 05 06 07 RRD(H) 10 9 8 7 6 5 4 3 2 1

For Ananda

This book is dedicated to
Robbie Flowers and Art Gabhart.
They bring the words to life every Sunday.

Contents

Thank-yous

To Koho Vince Anila because he read the renderings over and over without complaint, editing and making suggestions throughout. To Andrea Pedolsky because she is our guardian angel. To Renee Sedliar because she is a poet-editor with a big heart and a steady hand. To the Still Point sangha and especially the dharma students, who make this work gratifying. And to Ango Neil Heidrich because he is the embodiment of the bodhisattva of compassion.

Introduction

Twice in my life I've decided to give away everything I own, telling myself it's the Zen way—only to stall out at the bookcase. Both times I've been able to let go of everything except the books and, okay, a couple of pictures—paintings my mother has made for me and photographs of my family. Everything else goes. Even Buddha statues and birthday cards from my best friends. For the cards I just cross out my name and put in the name of whoever has a birthday coming up and/or could use a card with all the love it implies. Most recently that was my dharma brother Joe Sulak.

Attachments die hard. A few days ago I said to myself, "Okay, P'arang, this is it. You get to keep only one book. That's it. If you keep two you will end up in a hell realm. The worst one, the one where they burn people in boiling oil while cutting out eyes, and cutting off ears, nose, tongue, and brain." I figured I needed complete motivation.

Okay.

I choose the Dhammapada.

I'll keep it because it has never ever let me down. It's true north. I'll keep the Dhammapada because it makes me laugh at myself or sob at some karmic mess I've created. The Dhammapada oozes wisdom and compassion and reminds me that life is tough, that we all suffer, and that we do so because we insist on yearning for external stuff that won't ever make us permanently happy. It reminds me that enlightenment really is an inside job, one that includes letting go of the whole wildly entertaining melodrama I call my life.

The Dhammapada is a collection of more than four hundred Pali verses that Buddha is said to have spoken on over three hundred different occasions. Its first translation into a European language was by a Danish scholar, Victor Fausboll, in 1855. He translated it into Latin first, then German. In 1908 another scholar, Max Mueller, translated it into English. Between then and now dozens of versions, maybe more, have surfaced around the world. Because the eight or nine versions I've read have felt cumbersome for our inner-city sangha, about two years ago I decided to come up with a rendering just for us.

Still Point is located smack in the middle of rough-and-tumble downtown Detroit, a city of 140 acres and fewer people every year. Even with political pressure to increase the numbers, census-takers say that there are fewer than a million of us now. "According to the 2000 Census, [Detroit] has 6,855 residents per square mile, compared to 12,750 in Chicago, 26,403 in New York and 7,877 in sprawling Los Angeles."* The downsizing has left the city scarred. On one block, well-maintained homes. Across the street, windowless, burned-out homes fronted by porches that are falling apart and adorned with trash. The city says there are about eleven thousand of these buildings, including the city's historical train station, now so shattered you can see right through it on all of its floors. That's a conservative estimate,

---

* Jodi Wilgoren, "Detroit Urban Renewal Without the Renewal," *New York Times,* July 7, 2002, "National Report," p. 9.

though: anyone who lives here will argue that there are many more than eleven thousand buildings in trouble. "Kwame Kilpatrick, Detroit's young mayor, wants to tear them down: 'This is where drug dealers stash their drugs, this is where people stash guns, this is where girls get abused.'"*

On the other hand, we have a new $300 million baseball stadium right downtown, and rumors of further development keep increasing the value of the city's property. Still Point is on the corner of a pockmarked block, snuggled up against a street where people care for their buildings. Blight is the disease we watch. It's like a heart murmur that could kill us if we aren't really careful, if we don't change the way we live, if we don't take better care of each other.

We started the temple in September 2000, with yours truly as its first guiding teacher. I was coming off of five years as a dharma teacher in Ann Arbor, Michigan, where I had been sitting and training since 1988. Ordained in 1995, I fully expected to spend at least a few more years in Ann Arbor. But I parted ways with my teacher following a painful pilgrimage in Korea. Happily, he had managed to instill in me a deep love for the Korean Buddhist tradition by then. Our lineage is an earthy, colorful Zen with meditation at its core. Chanting, prostrations, and sutra study flesh out our spiritual practice. What emerges is a spontaneous, direct, and self-reliant style that's been in play since the fourteenth century, when a monk named T'aego formally unified all of the various Korean Zen sects under one roof. Days start early and end early, relative to Western standards. Every minute is a minute to awaken, and manual labor is encouraged, as are generosity and a big helping of humility.

---

* From the earlier-quoted *New York Times* article, p. 9.

When I decided it was time to leave Ann Arbor, I mentioned my decision to two friends who had started an organic bakery in the Cass Corridor of Detroit. In spite of many predictions of failure, they were thriving there. Their bakery, Avalon International Breads, is now a Detroit hotspot, and I can only imagine the number of "visionary" awards Jackie and Ann have hanging on their walls by now.

Anyway, they invited me to move to the corridor. After a business meeting in early spring of 2000, I went to see their new house, one of two brownstones still left standing in the neighborhood. On the top floor was a beautiful octagonal-shaped room.

"For your sangha," Jackie said.

I said yes to their suggestion and have never looked back. (Okay, maybe once, but that's because the neighborhood still doesn't have a decent bookstore.) Instead of the brownstone, we moved into the yoga room of the First Unitarian Universalist Church. It's been a wonderful home, even with no air-conditioning and eratic heat.

The people who come to Still Point are artists, entrepreneurs, students, health-care workers. Unemployed, homeless, homemakers. We're not a fancy crowd. As far as I can tell there isn't a millionaire in the bunch. Most weeks there isn't even a thousandaire. It's a group that wants solid spiritual advice. Forget esoteric; they want to know how to stop being furious with a boss who has an entire tree stuck up her butt.

When I decided that we needed a modernized version of the Dhammapada, Still Point's senior dharma student, Koho Vince Anila, said he'd help me come up with a rendering that would ring true to Detroit. For one thing, all the pronouns in all the versions I knew were masculine, and that just didn't work for contemporary life. And some of the metaphors used made me squint in concentration as I tried to understand their teaching. The version that we used as our starting point—our baseline Dhammapada, if you will—is *The Illustrated Dhammapada,* by Venerable Weragoda Sarada Maha Thero, published in Singapore and intentionally not copyrighted so that it could be available to a wide audience. It's a sweet, straightforward rendering of the verses. After over a year of playing with the lines, rewriting them, and reading them every Sunday at Still Point to make sure they made sense to people, we now offer them to you. I eat all blame for any hiccups and bumpy parts in our rendering and bow to the ground in gratitude to whoever carved the first version on a leaf so that the rest of us would have Buddha's words as a refuge thousands of years later.

Each chapter of *The Still Point Dhammapada* starts with a series of verses and then moves into a story relating to those verses. The stories underline at least one of the key teachings of the chapter, demonstrating the pertinence of Buddha's wisdom even today. The purpose of the stories is to offer an opening, one way to think about how to reflect Buddha's teachings in our own lives. There are countless other ways, though. Mostly the stories are about people who make up the Still Point sangha. How lucky I am that they're in my life!

P'arang Geri Larkin
September 1, 2002

THE TWIN VERSES

Our minds create everything.
If we speak or act with an impure mind
suffering is as certain
as the wheel of a bike that moves
when we start to pedal.

In the same way
if we speak or act with a pure mind
happiness will be ours—
a shadow that never leaves.

"He abused me; he beat me; he defeated me;
he robbed me."
If we cling to such thoughts
we live in hate.

"She abused me; she beat me; she defeated me;
she robbed me."
If we release such thoughts
our hate dissolves.

Hatred has never stopped hatred.
Only love stops hate.
This is the eternal law.

So many people fail to realize that
in quarreling
we ourselves are destroyed.

Those who recognize
this truth
restrain their quarrels.

If we live our lives obsessing
about pleasant things,
our senses unrestrained—
eating too much, being lazy—
temptations will destroy us
even as the wind
uproots a weak tree.

On the other hand,
if we are heedful,
restrain our senses,
keep our consumption moderate,
have faith in the Dharma—
and in ourselves—
if we are humble
and abide in our spiritual path,
temptation cannot destroy us
any more than the wind can overturn
a mountain.

A person without integrity,
who has no self-control,
who cannot be truthful,
is not worthy of wearing the yellow robe
of a monk.

Yet one who
keeps his word,
who practices self-control
and lives truthfully,
is worthy of wearing
the monk's robe.

If we mistake the unessential
for the essential
and the essential
for the unessential
we can never realize enlightenment.

Only when we see the essential as essential
and the unessential as unessential
can we fall into awakeness.

Even as rain penetrates a poorly roofed house
so does lust
for things, people, and experiences
penetrate an untrained mind.
But rain cannot penetrate
a well-roofed house,
and desire cannot penetrate
a well-trained mind.

The person who gives in to impure thoughts
suffers in this lifetime and beyond.
She suffers
greatly
when she sees
the mistakes she has made.

But if she does good deeds
she is joyful
in this life and beyond.
Seeing the purity of her deeds
she rejoices greatly.

Evildoers suffer now and later.
Realizing that they have been evil,
they suffer.
Even later evildoers suffer
from remorse
and wave upon wave of woe.

Those who perform good deeds
do not experience remorse and woe.
Instead
they are happy now
and they are happy later—
in this world
and the next
they know bliss.

You can recite all the sacred texts you want
but if you do not act accordingly

how will you benefit?
Without actions we are like
accountants
who count the wealth of others
but have little of their own.
We will not share the fruits of a holy life—
not ever.

Those who act
from compassion and wisdom—
however many holy texts they read—
those who let go of
greed, hatred, and delusion,
those who let go of all clinging,
who are able to follow the path to freedom
and know peace;
these are the ones
who will share the fruit
of the holy life.

"Are You Nuts?"

Melanie and I are sitting at the kitchen table, overwhelmed. "This is too much," we both think. The trash strewn all over this block alone is more than we can keep up with, even if we do a garbage pickup every morning instead of once a week.

On the nights when I'm awake at three A.M., I can stand at my bedroom window and watch drug transactions across the side street. I'm pretty sure it's cocaine changing hands, but it could be heroin. The water main on the front sidewalk sprang a leak recently, and it took ten days for city workers to show up to repair it, leaving us with a growing floodwater to jump across each morning to get to our respective cars. The security guys didn't show up for weeks to set up the system in Melanie's first-floor bedroom windows. Ango, our abbot, had to call them a lot. Only when he phoned to tell them how sad their response was making him did anyone appear at our door. And then they charged us an hourly rate that would have made a corporate attorney proud.

The view beyond our front porch is of an abandoned apartment house. It's four-storied, with boarded up windows, mostly. Graffiti galore. Weeds and trash surrounding it. Behind it, smelling like a dead animal, an overgrown vacant lot the size of four football fields. Behind the field, a huge eight-lane highway. We can hear the traffic through the night.

And yet.

Shunryu Suzuki once advised his students to "shine one corner." We can't solve the problems of Detroit from our little corner. But we can pick up the trash—for a quarter of the block anyway. And we can say good morning to everyone we see, and mean it. We can take a freshly baked pie to our neighbor, a nurse who works the midnight shift, and we can chant for peace and pure awakeness for all beings during evening practice.

When we first started Still Point Zen Buddhist Temple, in the fall of 2000, well-intentioned friends outside of Detroit warned me about moving into such a dangerous neighborhood. Inner-city Detroit. The Cass Corridor. Were we nuts?

Hate never dispels hate.

Move in we did. Replaced a bullet-shattered billboard in the front of the temple with new glass. It's still there, hole-free. Started picking up the garbage on the church lawn and haven't stopped. Hung chimes—beautiful, expensive chimes—on a tree branch at the temple's front door. Anyone could steal them. No one has.

Started building stupas, small piles of rocks, to remind ourselves that enlightenment can happen at any time, anywhere, and that every place is a sacred space. The stupas are still standing.

Then, in July 2001, we bought a building for an abbey, a big old brick house, a house with ten bedrooms and at least fourteen years of neglect. It's a ten-minute walk from the temple, past the abandoned apartment house, the field, and the highway. Two Dumpsters' worth of garbage went out the abbey's front door in the first two weeks. A "freebie" garage sale was available to anyone who would haul stuff away. We started scraping and painting. For days at a time one person or another, all but one of them volunteers, stood on too-high ladders trying to get the house's wood trim painted before the first frost.

A printing company made a huge peace pole for the front lawn. It stands about eight feet tall and has spiritual instructions carved into it in big red letters. "Pay attention!" "Do no harm!" "Just this moment!" "Only do good!" Every day someone from the neighborhood stops to read the words, looks up at the house, smiles—usually a curious smile—and walks on.

For our first two months in the abbey a man stood in front of the house for about an hour every afternoon. He was waiting for a bus. He never smiled. His face was so disfigured—by a bullet wound, it looked like—that he wouldn't even turn to fully face the house when he watched us painting, cleaning, and sorting. Almost every day, for one reason or another, I walked past him. Sometimes it was to throw something into the dumpster. Sometimes it was to carry a ladder to the back of the house, or to paint. Sometimes I was racing to the hardware store before it closed because someone needed a particular tool to keep going.

He always felt pretty angry when I passed. I'd say hi anyway. We all did. But he never smiled. Never responded. Sometimes someone'd add, "How are you today?" knowing there wasn't going to be an answer.

Then one day the man didn't show up. He was gone for a month, and we missed him. Even though he'd never spoken, he'd still been company.

Just as suddenly as he'd disappeared, he came back one Wednesday afternoon. Because the day was noticeably colder and shorter than the last time I'd seen him, I was concentrating on finishing the painting of the porch ceiling. Moving too fast for myself I was making a mess, wasting paint and time as I stopped to clean up after myself by the half-hour. Curses started showing up, first in my mind and then out of my mouth. I kept going anyway, knowing it would be spring before we could paint again. Five months away.

Just as the sun went down, making it too dark to see, I finished the last corner. A clean gray porch ceiling—slate gray—was ready for winter. Rushing down the walk to put the ladder away I almost slammed into the man.

Skidding to a stop I smiled, glad to see him.

"Hi."

He looked at me for what felt like forever. I suddenly realized that he had heard me swearing, especially the "Sweet Mary Joseph Jesus" that I'd learned from my Irish grandmother at the ripe old age of five.

"I've been watching you. You're doing good work."

And he smiled back at me for the first time.

Only love dispels hate. This is the eternal law.

Now when we see him, which isn't very often, this man tells us about the neighborhood, its history and people. One day he told me all about his hopes for Detroit, for the children; told me how it could be the city of the future, with its potential. He's right, of course. And he's a wonderful storyteller, knows the juiciest stories, the ones about the prostitutes who used to live in our house, and the ones about the children who filled it when it was an orphanage. He knows the heartbreaks and the miracles and who used to live with whom and who's been fighting since grade school. Next time I see him, maybe he'll come in for tea.

2

HEEDFULNESS

Heedfulness is the path to the deathless;
inattention the path to death.
The heedful do not die.
Those who are inattentive are already dead.

Understanding this,
the wise rejoice in heedfulness.

The woman who is constantly heedful
is freed.
The man who is constantly heedful
is freed.
Both attain Nirvana.

Happiness steadily increases for the person
who is energetic, heedful,
pure in conduct,
and kind.

Persevere.
With your sustained effort,

earnestness,
discipline,
and self-control,
you will make for yourself an island
which no flood can destroy.

Fools indulge in inattention
while the wise guard their heedfulness
as the most important thing in their lives.

Do not lose your focus.
Do not become inattentive.
Do not let yourself become addicted
to sensual pleasures.

In the strength of your resolve
you will discover true bliss.

Replacing inattention
with heedfulness,
the wise woman is free from sorrow.
From her place of wisdom
she can see the sorrows of the world.

Heedful among the inattentive,
watchful among the sleeping,
the wise man surpasses the foolish man
just as a young racehorse outruns an old steed.

Through heedfulness Indra became
king of the gods.

Attention is always praised.
Inattention is always blamed.

The person on a spiritual path
who delights in heedfulness
and fears inattention
advances like fire,
burning everything
that is holding her back.

The person on a spiritual path
who delights in heedfulness
and fears inattention
cannot fail.
He has found the path to happiness.

Shine One Corner

Ango is twenty-eight, I think. He seems younger. It's the way he moves, almost like a puppy. Tall, lanky, sweet, wool-capped most of the winter. Full of shiny-eyed grins. When I met him in the summer of 2000 he was thinking about going to Korea as a novice monk. The previous year had been hard for him. A house fire had burned up everything but his camera and backpack. Did I know of any monasteries that would accept a Westerner? Only one.

Then he was gone. He had escaped on a jet. I figured that Korea and he had finally met.

Two months later we opened Still Point Temple, and there was Ango at one of the first services. He kept coming back week after week. Front row. A year later when an announcement was made that we were buying an old orphanage for an abbey, Ango was the first person to sign up as a resident.

None of us knew how much sheer physical labor it would take to make the building clean, let alone livable. Peeling walls, crumbling stairs, bathroom pipes that led to nowhere. After a month of dawn-to-dark work, I for one was desperate for short-cuts. One back bedroom had a faded, scarred wooden floor. In-expensive carpet would mean that we wouldn't have to look at it. I started looking for cheap rugs, figuring we'd forget that the wood was under there after a while. Without saying much Ango decided to refinish the floor on his own. It took two weeks of painstaking, back-crunching work. Floor sanders are unbelievably heavy, and they have a willpower of their own. The only way to keep them aimed in the direction you want is to hunch over them and use all your strength to keep them steady. Back muscles don't have a chance. But Ango stuck with it. The room is now one of the prettiest in the house.

Another massive project was the abbey bathroom. It was as big as a small bedroom, complete with a claw-footed bathtub and the ugliest plastic flooring this side of the Rockies. Yellow with a black diamond pattern. Fifty years earlier the yellow had probably been white. Now, though, it looked as if a thousand kittens had peed on it and nobody had bothered to clean up after them. The room even had an unmistakable kitten pee smell.

Ango announced that he wanted to pull up a corner of the flooring to see what was under it. Wood. By then five of us were living in the house, with four of us sharing the bathroom. Would we mind if he took a long weekend to tear up the flooring and refinish the floor?

We agreed.

But remodeling projects are remodeling projects, and a day becomes a week, and wooden floors have rotten spots. By day four the rest of us were antsy. Let's just cover it up with some cheap tiling. Despite our complaints, though, Ango kept going, kept doing the next task, kept his eye on the wooden planks, the image of a hardwood floor dancing in his head. On some days the next task meant driving twenty miles to the nearest Home Depot to rent a sander. Sometimes it meant spending three hours scrubbing a twelve-inch patch of linoleum glue off the wood.

"Happiness steadily increases for the person
who is energetic, heedful,
pure in conduct,
and kind."

Every once in a while I would stand at the bathroom door and watch Ango. He rarely noticed, his mindfulness was so strong. The times he did notice, he would look up, grin a great grin, and keep working at the same steady pace. As the few days stretched into a few weeks, he never lost his mindfulness, never sped up just to "get things done."

Even when he had to get plumbers in to rehook the toilet to our ancient piping, Ango held his pace and kept an eye out for problem areas.

As soon as the floor was sanded and polished, the rest of us called the room done. Not Ango. He kept going. He cut some edging for where the floor meets the walls. Took a day to do it because he wanted to make certain that the fit was right. Stained it to match the hue of the floor. Another day. Then spent a Sunday putting it in.

Now the abbey has a beautiful bathroom. Quiet. Serene. Earth tones top to bottom. Not to brag, but I'm sure that Martha Stewart would approve. And Buddha would smile. Even friends outside of the sangha want to come to the abbey to take a bath here. It's that wonderful, this ode to heedfulness.

"He has found the path to happiness."

3

THE MIND
A flickering, fickle mind
is difficult to control.
The wise person strengthens it
with determination.

Like a fish
thrown onto the shoreline,
the mind thrashes and quivers
when we do not transcend passions.

The mind is difficult to control.
It flies from object to object,
landing wherever it pleases.
Thus it is good to tame the mind,
for a well-tamed mind brings happiness.

The mind is also very difficult to perceive
because it can be subtle—
moving all over the place,
stopping wherever it pleases.
A wise man guards his mind,
knowing that a guarded mind brings happiness.

The mind, quieted, frees us
from all delusions.

A person whose mind is not steadfast,
whose confidence wavers,
who does not know how
to quiet her mind,
will never know perfect wisdom.

But a person whose mind is quiet and clear—
who has transcended good and evil—
for such a vigilant one
there is no fear.

Knowing how fragile our bodies are,
we need to make a fortress of our minds.
In this way
when temptation strikes
wisdom is the weapon that will defend us
from anger,
greed, and delusion.

Before long our bodies,
deprived of consciousness,
will lie on the earth,
discarded like unwanted appliances.

Your own mind,
untamed,
can harm you more than
anyone or anything,
even your own worst enemy.

Neither your mother nor your father
nor any relative
can help you more than
your own mind
when it is calm and clear.
Direct it toward good.

Boot Camp for Buddhists

One of Still Point's jewels is a dharma student named Ron Allen. He's a big, handsome African-American, a Detroit Detroiter. Grew up in the hood and has a heart as big as the universe. In the two years that I've known him I've never heard him say an unkind word, though he's had plenty of opportunities. About six years ago Ron decided that he didn't want to be addicted to heroin anymore. Now he does prison dharma and recovery work when he isn't writing poetry or producing plays. If the MacArthur Foundation ever sniffed around Detroit, he'd be an obvious choice for a genius grant. He's that good.

Ron is one of Detroit's best-loved artists. A homegrown hero. At first, whenever I saw him he was with two or three people, usually talking poetry. Without my knowing, he was also watching Still Point. It was an honor when he applied to be a seminarian. Since Buddhism was pretty new to him, I wasn't sure how he'd fare.

The answer? Buddhism and Ron Allen are a match made in heaven.

Retreats are a way of life at Still Point. One-day retreats happen on the first Saturday of the month, except for August and January. In the spring and fall we have three-day retreats. Between Christmas and New Year and again at the end of June, five-day retreats.

I honestly thought it would take a while for people to start signing up for these sessions once we started offering them. Retreats are tough. Backs just plain ache. Entire legs go to sleep from the sitting postures. It's impossible to escape from moods, including festering ones like anger, worry, and guilt.

From the start, though, people showed up for the experience of sitting for at least one full day. For the longer retreats, many of us get up at four A.M. to start sitting. Then each day turns into "boot camp for Buddhists." A pattern of thirty-minute sittings is broken up by ten-minute breaks, walking meditation, and work practice until ten P.M., when the formal day ends. Even then a handful of people always keep going, trading the opportunity to sleep for yet more meditation.

At the three- and five-day retreats, teaching interviews with the guiding teacher are offered every morning and most evenings. Actually, the word *offered* is euphemistic in the extreme. Not only are all of the retreatants *expected* to come to an interview; they're expected to practically *run* into the interview room, eager to experience whatever is sitting there waiting for them.

We line up for interviews in groups of five. At the sound of the first bell, the senior dharma student rushes for the stairs, headed for the interview room. As soon as his interview is over the bell rings twice and the next person in line lunges for the stairs, braced for his turn. Hearts beat wildly while we wait. What will happen behind that door?

Sometimes it's a simple instruction about practice: "Just be your practice." Or "Take refuge in your breathing." Sometimes a hwadu or koan (a Zen riddle) is asked: "What was your face before your parents were born?" or "What is Buddha?"

Sometimes as soon as the person sits on her cushion, facing the teacher, a bell is rung without any dialogue at all.

In the interviews most people reflect on the difficulties they're having controlling their thoughts. People typically find that they can sit quietly for one, five, seven minutes, and then—wham! They're off into the land of planning or worrying or fantasy or fear. Always the response is to just "do your practice," and when you catch your mind wandering simply bring it back to the breath. Just come back to the breath all hundred thousand times. Eventually your mind will tire of wandering off. Eventually.

On retreat evenings, the interviews are a little different. The sole purpose of these "thirty-second interviews" is to infuse energy into quickly tiring body-minds. During evening sessions the retreatants all know ahead of time the question they'll be asked in the interview. Sometimes it's: "Can you work harder?" Sometimes, "Are you awake?" Sometimes, "Are you doing your best?"

Then, one by one, each person runs up the stairs at the sound of the bell, sits on the interview cushion, shouts his or her answer, and races back down the stairs and into the meditation hall to continue sitting.

The winter retreat of 2001 was Ron's first long retreat. I wasn't sure how he would do, since it promised to be grueling and he was still recovering from foot surgery. But he showed up, sat down in a chair, faced the wall, and didn't budge. Mountains and rivers were Ron, and he was mountains and rivers.

> "A flickering, fickle mind
> is difficult to control.
> The wise person strengthens it
> with determination."

On the second night of the retreat, the interview question was, "Are you doing your best?" Most of the retreatants shouted

"Yes!" or "I could do better!" (though one of the dharma students shouted, "Damned if I know!" which practically brought the house down).

Then came Ron.

He ran up the stairs. Sat on his cushion and in one breath shouted, "I am doing my best! I am not doing my best!"

Yes! He had it! The mind moves all over the place. Flickering. Fickle. His practice was strong enough to let him see, clearly, how fast his mind was moving, bouncing from one end of the universe to the other end in less than an instant.

In that watchfulness, real spiritual work can be done—the taming, the comforting, the quieting of our minds until finally (maybe out of sheer exhaustion) samadhi kicks in. And we know in our bones that behind all of that junk mail we call *thinking* is Buddha.

4

FLOWERS
Who shall see the true nature
of this world of temptation?
Who will investigate the Dharma
as carefully as an excellent florist
chooses flowers?

A person sincere about his spiritual practice
will see the true nature
of this world of temptation.

Knowing that this body
is nothing but
a mirage,
one should cut the flowers of desire
and, through such effort,
escape death.

The woman who gathers the flowers of desire,
whose mind clings to pleasures,
is carried off by death in the same way
that a sleeping village
is swept away by a great flood.

The man who gathers the flowers of desire,
whose mind clings to pleasure,
is overpowered by death
in the same way.

As a bee gathers nectar from a flower
without marring the blossom's beauty or scent,
so should a spiritual seeker
wander through the world.

Do not analyze the failings of others.
Instead look at your own failings.
Where have you been responsible?
Where have you been irresponsible?

Like those flowers that are beautiful
but scentless
are the beautiful but empty words
of those who do not practice
what they say.

Like the flowers
that are beautiful and fragrant
are the wisdom-filled words
of those who practice
what they teach.

Like garlands
woven from carefully chosen blooms,
fashion your life
from constant good deeds.

The perfumes of sandalwood and jasmine
drift with the wind.
Their scents are faint compared to
the perfume of the virtuous.
It fills the sky even against the wind,
even to the heavens.

Temptation never blocks the path
of people who practice virtue,
paying attention to their thoughts
and their actions.
The practice of virtue protects them
and opens a path to enlightenment.

Just like a sweet-smelling lotus
that grows out of the mud
of a silty pond,
a sincere spiritual seeker
outshines those steeped in ignorance
with a wisdom that reflects the moon's bright light.

Buddhas Blooming

Still Point has a three-year seminary. The regimen is tough. Six mornings a week students get up early to do 108 prostrations (or full bows to the floor). Then they sit for thirty minutes, after which there is chanting. Throughout the day, more chanting—at least thirty-three rounds of the three refuges:

> I go to Buddha as my refuge.
> I go to Dharma as my refuge.
> I go to Sangha as my refuge.

At night, more sitting, more chanting, and study. First-year students read about Buddha's life and his disciples. In the second year the students face off with key teachings: the Diamond Sutra, various Perfect Wisdom Sutras, and the Platform Sutra of the Third Patriarch. By the third year the students are learning about different Buddhist lineages and reading books such as *The Training of the Zen Buddhist Monk* by D. T. Suzuki and *Thousand Peaks: Korean Zen Tradition and Teachers* by Mu Soeng Sunim. On Sundays, for at least three hours, students help with services and tasks that need doing. If we have a retreat, I expect to see them in attendance. If someone asks for a presentation about Buddhism, ditto. Twice a year they write essays about some aspect of Buddhism. (This year the essays have been mostly summaries of the readings, because everyone has had such busy lives.)

The people who have stepped forward to be in the seminary give me hope—for Detroit, for Dharma, for the world. To a person, they are moral, lively, and determined. Koho is a writer, a poet, a wanderer, someone who lights up a room with his presence. If he wasn't doing dharma he would make a great stand-up comedian. Kogam, a veterinarian, was in a Christian seminary prior to joining Still Point. He is upright and beautiful. Sarah is a teacher, a poet, a mother, a carpenter. She is calm and sweet, always. Ron is our resident poet and playwright, Joe is Detroit's urban forester, and Cat, a student and massage therapist who can work magic on an exhausted body. Detroiters all. Rodger, sweet and quiet and steady, drives up from West Virginia.

All students are required to take the precepts: not to harm; not to take what isn't given; not to lie; not to muddy one's mind (particularly with drugs and/or alcohol); not to be sexually promiscuous. Students are also expected to follow the spirit of the Six Paramitas:

May I be generous and helpful.

May I be pure and virtuous.

May I be patient. May I be able to bear and forbear the wrongs of others.

May I be strenuous, energetic, and persevering.

May I practice meditation and attain concentration and oneness to serve all beings.

May I gain wisdom and be able to give the benefit of my wisdom to others.

I watch the group grow, and each student bloom, week by week. Every obligation is performed with unfailing cheerfulness—even, sometimes, eagerness. Except for one thing: keeping a journal.

Six days a week students are required to reflect and report in their journal on five items:

- Their practice

- Time spent in idle chitchat

- Particular resistance to their practice

- What troubled them most that day

- What made them happy that day

The journal creates more problems for the students than any other obligation. Every week, two or three journals fall by the wayside, entry-free. In the winter months when we're all distracted by the difficulties of short, dark, cold days, there are even more empty journals than usual. One of the students had such a strong resistance to journaling that someone finally suggested he simply put a thumbs-up or thumbs-down sign at the end of each of the five points.

I struggled with the same issue when I was in the seminary. For the entire first year my answers were limited to one or two words. Only when one of my dharma sisters suggested that I was missing a real opportunity to be more mindful did I start to write longer answers—sometimes as much as a paragraph—for each point of reflection. Only then did I see my own patterns of resistance: How I planned to do too much every day so that I would have a legitimate reason not to write an entry at night. How I was troubled with lots of emotions—not just worry and anxiety, but nuances of both, along with sadness and sometimes even jealousy. The paragraphs showed me that all sorts of things made me happy—not just finishing a project or spending time with my children. Suddenly happiness included the sounds of birds, the smell of incense, the feel of a quilt.

Mostly what I learned was how unmindful I was, and how quickly my desires morphed into obsessions. A flash of hunger and the next thing I knew I wasn't just making a bowl of soup; I was driving to Ben and Jerry's. A flash of my boyfriend and suddenly I was wondering where he was, who he was with, and why he hadn't called that day. The journal forced me to observe my own river of thinking. As I did, I realized that I could actually let go of thoughts that I knew were only going to spiral downhill into a sewer of neuroses. As a result I was better able to balance my life, to take both it and me less seriously. I saw my workaholic nature but also recognized how I put off exercise out of sheer laziness (even though I loved it once I got my butt in gear). I saw how lucky I was and what amazing friends I have and how incredibly beautiful Michigan is, season after season.

So we have journals at Still Point. And we write in them when our yearning for spiritual growth outweighs our resistance to writing. Always, watching our minds and noting our patterns, we are helped. Not happy each minute maybe, but definitely more sane.

They are beautiful flowers, blooming, this group. Their journals prove it.

THE FOOL
The night is long for the sleepless.
The road is long for the weary.
The wandering through lives
is endless
for someone who misses the point
of his life:
spiritual practice.

If you cannot find your equal or better
to go with you,
then travel alone
rather than spend time with a fool.

"I have children.
I have wealth."
Thus the ignorant person thinks she is secure.
Indeed, she herself is not permanent.
How can her children or wealth be permanent?

Seeing her own foolishness
a person becomes wise,

while the fool who thinks she is wise
remains a fool.

Fools spend their entire lives
exposed to wisdom
and still do not understand the Dharma
any more than a spoon can taste soup.

A wise man, even if he associates with
an enlightened person only for a moment,
will recognize the Dharma
just as the tongue knows the taste of soup.

Fools are their own enemies,
performing evil deeds
which bear bitter outcomes.

You know when a deed is harmful.
You regret doing it and, with tears,
reap its fruit.

A deed is good when it is not regretted.
Happiness
accompanies its fruition.
An evil deed may seem
as sweet as honey
until it is played out.
When that happens
the fool grieves deeply.

As a form of spiritual practice,
for months a fool may fast—

eating only as much food
as can be balanced
on the tine of a fork.

It does not matter.
Her effort is worthless
compared to the
actions of a person
who understands the path to peace.

Like milk,
evil deeds do not sour immediately.
Instead, the souring follows the fool
through time,
hidden until it ripens.

Knowledge and fame are the ruination of a fool.
Pride destroys the fool's illumination.
It destroys her wisdom.

A fool wants recognition,
praise for qualities he does not have,
authority over others,
and honor from people
near and far.

"Let people think
things happen because of me.
Let them obey me in all ways
great and small."
These are the thoughts of a fool
whose conceit grows.

The truth is that one path leads to
worldly gain;
another, to enlightenment.
Knowing this, those who are
students of Buddha
train themselves
not to delight so much
in the favors of the world,
but to stay detached.

Crazy Wisdom

"The night is long for the sleepless.
The road is long for the weary.
The wandering through lives
is endless
for someone who misses the point
of his life:
spiritual practice."

In our Korean Zen Buddhist lineage, there is a library's worth of stories of crazy wisdom. People who appear to be wise aren't. People who act crazy or sound crazy are in reality great teachers. Holy places are tourist traps. Tiny buildings tucked into the mountains are holy places.

When I moved into the Ann Arbor Zen Buddhist Temple years ago, there was one story I asked to hear over and over—like a child asking for a favorite bedtime book. It was about renovating one of Samu Sunim's first temples in Toronto. Sunim would accept help from anyone. Most of the people who showed up on his doorstep were young construction workers and artists, and their mates. They would work from dawn to dusk on the building. Quite often a man recently released from a local mental institution would walk by the building, sometimes stopping to watch. Sunim eventually asked him to help.

The man accepted and proceeded to drive everyone else nuts. He didn't do things the way anyone else did. Argued a lot. Made mistakes. Smelled like a garbage dump. The other workers complained about him. They begged Sunim to tell the man to go away. He wouldn't, though. And yet when the man eventually *did* leave (it turned out that even Sunim had his limits), people couldn't believe how much they missed him. He had forced them to be mindful, generous, and patient. He had provided an unending stream of humor and wackiness. One of the sangha members even went looking for the guy, realizing that they had lost a great teacher.

Starting Still Point, I wondered if we would be as lucky. Then I met Art Gabhart. Within a month of deciding that Detroit was going to be my future, I got a furious phone call at home from him, at that time a complete stranger. "Why are you coming to Detroit?" It was a shout. His voice was angry. "Because I was invited," I replied. "Oh," the voice said. And hung up. My first introduction to Art.

Art is unlike anyone I've ever met. A hard-core Detroiter, he does things when he wants to do them. Not before. Not after. Sometimes he promises to do projects that he then leaves undone. At other times he takes on chores that nobody else has even noticed need doing. When visitors were coming from New York City once, he put brass numbers next to the front door of the abbey to make sure that the guests would be able to find us. Handmade a wood backing for them. It took two days. Plus he made the doorbell work, mostly. Another day of work.

When we had a Mountain Seat Ceremony to honor Ango Neil Heidrich as our first abbot at the abbey—the same Ango who had so painstakingly refinished our bathroom floor—Art was the person who drove across the border to Windsor to get Vietnamese spring rolls for him. None of the rest of us had a passport or birth certificate available to show the border patrol.

Arthur started to fix the ceiling in our kitchen one day when the sagging tiles caught his eye. That job still isn't finished. On the other hand, he spent days jacking up falling-down stairs on the other side of the house so that we could use them without falling through.

I mostly can't walk through a room without Arthur's asking me a question about the Dharma. What does the hand mudra where one hand is up like a stop sign mean? What do I think of a particular sutra? (Invariably one I've never heard of.) What is the Buddhist take on emptiness? Did Nansen really kill the cat? (This from a famous Zen riddle about a monk who killed a cat.) Even setting up a weekly one-on-one meeting for the single purpose of answering his questions doesn't stop the stream. I almost never know the answers, because the questions are often about specific details related to the life of a particular bodhisattva or a Zen master. Maybe I've had two correct responses in the last year. Those were sheer luck.

Arthur's spiritual practice is strong and his heart is huge. When I feel myself getting angry at his questions or at jobs not done and hear myself talking to him through teeth clenched with frustration, his reaction is always completely open. He listens to my words. Then there's silence. Then, "My mistake was . . ."—even when I'm the one who's wrong, which happens sometimes. And I realize how much inside spiritual work I have left to do until I can be that spontaneous, until I can instantly respond to someone else's anger with, "My mistake was . . ."

If Arthur ever left the sangha, I'd go hunt for him.

THE WISE
A wise person who admonishes
you for your faults
is a good person to follow.
Following such a one is like
following a guide to a buried treasure.
Simply being
with that person
is helpful to you.

Let the wise woman
advise and instruct;
let her
dissuade you from that
which is wrong.
Such a woman is held dear
by the good;
she is disliked
only by the bad.

Do not spend
time with evil friends

or with people who are mean.
Instead
associate with those
who are noble.

He who drinks deeply of the Dharma
lives happily.
His mind is tamed.
In fact, the wise
delight in the Dharma
as it is revealed to them.

As a farmer channels water
and carpenters shape wood,
so the wise tame their minds.

In the same way that a solid rock
is unshaken by the wind,
the wise are unshaken
by praise
and blame.

Just as a deep lake is
clear and still,
the wise,
on hearing the teachings,
become filled with peace.

The wise give up
their attachments to everything.
Unshaken by craving,
they are calm with feelings
of both pleasure and pain.

Unjust means are never used
by the wise
to obtain success,
children, wealth, or land.
In fact, unjust means are *never* used—
even for the sake of others.

Few people are able to cross the shore to
    enlightenment.
Most spend their lives
running up and down the shoreline
on this side.

But those who practice
according to the Dharma
will awaken.
They will be able
to swim across the river
of passions, a river
difficult to cross.

The wise woman,
giving up craving
with enlightenment as her goal,
must give up all dark states
and cultivate pure, good ones.

She should seek
great delight in solitude
and detachment.
She should let go
of sensual pleasures

and, clinging to nothing,
cleanse herself
of all mental impurities.

The people whose minds
are well developed in
the Factors of Enlightenment
and who have rid themselves
of all craving
rejoice in their abandonment
of grasping.

Such people,
with all defilements
eradicated,
are powerful.
They have awakened in this world.

Being Upright

When I gave my last dharma talk at the Ann Arbor Zen Buddhist Temple before heading east to Detroit, its resident priest, one of my dharma sisters, gave me a card signed by many of the temple members. On it were these words:

> Go now, and wander
> for the welfare of many, out of compassion
> for the world.
> For the benefit, welfare
> and happiness of
> gods and all beings.
> Teach the Dharma that
> is good in the beginning,
> good in the middle
> and good in the end.
> —*the Buddha*

At that time there were only four of us going to the city— Koho Vince Anila, Sanch'on Amy Park, Michael Fuhrman, and I. Zen warriors ready to fall in love with a new community. Enough of Ann Arbor's university town life. Detroit Zen City was calling our names. At the time there was only one other Zen center near Detroit—in Hamtramck, actually—a small and intense center taught by a rugged, demanding Zen Buddhist monk. There wasn't anything in the heart of the city, nothing near the university, nothing accessible to beginners looking for their first three-dimensional taste of Zen.

I expected that there would be problems as we settled in. We were moving into a tough neighborhood, after all. There would be drugs, and the homeless people had a reputation for being pretty aggressive. The first piece of advice I got, walking into the Unitarian Church on Cass Avenue (which would become our first temple), was to make sure not to leave anything of value visible in my car. The windshield shards I walked across coming up the walk were visible proof that the advice needed heeding.

I expected to see mental illness as well. Michigan doesn't house the mentally ill much. Maybe not at all by the time you read this. Sure enough, a handful of paranoid schizophrenics gradually came our way. They take turns coming to services now. As long as they can sit quietly and have taken a bath or shower in the past twenty-four hours or so they're welcome. Mild urine smell is good for concentration practice.

What I didn't expect was the sheer toughness of Detroit. Within weeks we had lost a young man to a heroin overdose. Many of the sangha members are recovering from some addiction. In fact, if we include being addicted to living, it's all of us. Mainly, though, people struggle with drugs, alcohol, cigarettes, food, gambling. (In an effort to throw some positive energy into the wind, we purposefully moved close to one of the handful of new casinos that have popped up in the past three years.)

Nor did I expect to get vicious emails from people blaming Still Point, and sometimes me personally, for everything from destroying marriages to bringing a new evil into Detroit, but those emails came. I didn't expect one of the seminary students to commit suicide, but he did. And I didn't expect to spend much of one night in an emergency room with a sweet and beautiful young woman who had talked openly about killing herself several times in a week. But that happened as well.

Two other young women needed a place to live. The man they lived with beat them, though they didn't say the words out loud.

I secretly asked Buddha for expandable walls at the abbey. "You're why we're here," I told him. "The least you can do is give us more space."

Twice so far I've called my dharma sister back in Ann Arbor for advice. "This is so much. How can I bear the heartbreak of all of it?" She listens and tells me to be upright.

Okay.

Being upright means staying smack dab in the middle of what's going on. No running away. No pretending that the situation is any different than it is. It means breathing in and out and listening to our heart. And asking only one question: What can I do right this minute? Sometimes I think of it as "mountain and river" practice. Detroit is all too often a mountain of heartbreaks and a river of sorrows. All I can do is look for cracks where some help can be offered. Sometimes I can only witness. Some days I can only pick up garbage or make the first call to a shelter or delete the email and chant for the person who wrote it.

My dharma sister is wise. She never lectures. She never blames or tells me where I've screwed up. She doesn't offer huge solutions or even the promise of a better tomorrow. Instead, simply by listening to me without judgments, she pulls me back to the moment where I can do "just this" practice until somehow the next step appears. Upright, I can—*we* can—allow ourselves to experience every single moment fully and directly. Each time I talk with her, her reaction opens up a feeling of okayness for me, of spaciousness and, of all things, joy. Joy in the middle of the whole crazy mess. I bow to the ground in gratitude for her wisdom.

THE WORTHY

The person who has gone
the distance,
who is sorrowless,
free of everything,
ties loosened—
in him the fever of passion
no longer exists.

The heedful strive diligently.
They take no delight in the home.
Like swans that forsake
a muddy pool they leave
their home life behind.

The worthy do not hoard.
When they eat,
they eat mindfully.
Their focus is on awakening—
an awakening that is signless.
Like the path of birds in the sky
their destination cannot be traced.

He whose defilements are destroyed,
she who is unattached to sustenance,
the ones who focus on
an awakening that is signless—
these have a path
that cannot be traced
just as a migrating bird
leaves no track.

She whose senses are subdued,
whose pride is destroyed,
who is free of corruption—
that woman is held dear
even by the gods.

One who is worthy is like the earth.
Even when provoked he does not respond in anger.
He is serene and pure
like a clear lake.
For him there will be no more
rebirth.

Calm is his mind.
Calm is his speech.
Calm is his action.
He is free, perfectly peaceful,
unshaken by the ups and downs of life.

The woman who is awake, wise,
free of attachments;
the woman who has shed her cravings—
she, indeed, is a supreme woman.

In the city or the town,
in the forest, valley, or hills,
wherever the worthy ones dwell
is delightful.

Delightful to the worthy
are the places where others
find no joy.
Being free of the pull of passions,
the worthy rejoice anywhere
precisely because
they seek no delight.

A Cat Named Ferlinghetti

At Still Point we do blessings for both children and pets. They're always touching services. In the presence of the baby or animal we vow to take refuge in Buddha, Dharma, and Sangha. We recite the precepts on behalf of the child or animal as well, promising that we will do our Buddha best to live ethical and moral lives on behalf of the child or pet.

Our first baby blessing was for Rafaela, the daughter of Ann and Jackie Perrault-Victor. At the end of a regular Sunday service, people were invited to walk up to the altar, where the baby was being held, to bow to her. It was a visible gesture of intention to keep the precepts in her name. We all cried when the first person to walk up the aisle was a troubled man who smelled so strongly of rotten garbage that three sticks of incense couldn't keep up with him. Rafaela now has the Buddhist name Tara. She already lights up the community with her laughter and adventurous nature and is destined to be a great woman, modeled after her mothers.

For a long time nobody requested a pet blessing. I was surprised. After all, this is a sangha of animal lovers, animal rights activists, and veterinarians. Finally one Sunday, Suzanne Sunflower approached me after the five P.M. service. Suzanne is quiet, tall, beautiful. A writer. She's lived in the Cass Corridor for years, in a building that—I admit it—made me take a deep breath when I first walked in. Dark and looming, maybe ten stories high, the building sits across the street from a church that provides daily lunches for the homeless community. Bars guard everything that opens, and names have been left off the buzzers. The way I found Suzanne's apartment was by asking people going in and out of the building if they knew her. Finally, someone did. A big, burly man hauling furniture out of a side door told me how to negotiate the stairs and hallways to get to her basement apartment.

Suzanne had asked me to do a pet blessing for her cat, Ferlinghetti. The tremor in her voice when she made her request was the first emotion I had seen in her. Typically she was very cool—a person you would want standing beside you in a crisis. Now, though, her cat was dying, and she wanted to honor him.

To prepare for a pet blessing I always ask for a description of the animal. What's he like? That background helps me to choose an appropriate Buddhist name for him during the ceremony. I asked Suzanne about Ferlinghetti. For a couple of Sundays she said nothing, and I concluded that she'd forgotten about the description. Just when I'd decided to ask her about him a second time, she handed me a sheet of lined notebook paper. On it she'd written:

FERLINGHETTI FACTS

1. Over the last fifteen years he's tolerated living with me in a tent in the desert and accompanied me on other such adventures.

2. He's alerted me to prowlers regularly.

3. He saved my life from fire in our home.

4. He's been completely faithful.

Ferlinghetti protected and comforted Suzanne. He knew how to help her, quietly and completely. He loved her without bounds, visibly and with deep loyalty.

When she told me not long after the blessing that he'd died, I cried for them both. We forget how much the animals of the earth protect and care for us—what wise beings they can be. I vowed to remember to protect and care for animals in return, even when it means waking up to a three A.M. mouse party above my head in the abbey attic. First thoughts waking up? "They're at it again!" Second thoughts waking up? Remembering Ferlinghetti and Suzanne and thinking how lucky we are to share this wild and crazy planet with so many other beings. They keep the earth spinning.

THE THOUSANDS

Though a thousand verses
of useless words may be offered,
better is a single sound that,
heard,
brings peace.

Though a thousand verses
of useless words may be offered,
better is a single verse that,
heard,
brings peace.

Though a hundred verses
of useless words may be recited,
it is better to listen to a single word of the Dharma.
This is where one finds peace.

Better than conquering
a million soldiers in a battle
is victory over oneself.

Self-conquest is a far greater victory
than conquering others.
No one, not even a demon,
can win back the victory
of such a person.
He is self-subdued.
She lives in continuous restraint.

You could make
a thousand sacrifices,
month after month,
for a hundred years
and not honor the teachings
as much as showing respect—
for a single moment—
to a person who has conquered
herself.

You could tend sacred fires in the woods
for a century
and not honor the teachings as deeply
as a moment of reverence
given to a person who has conquered
himself.

In this world the gifts
a person seeking merit might give
in a year
are not worth a fraction
of a moment's
reverence

to one who has conquered
herself.

Those in the habit of constantly
honoring and protecting people
whose spirituality has matured
experience the four blessings of
a long life, beauty, joy, and strength.

Better than a hundred years of
immorality and unrestraint
is a single day
in the life of one who is moral
and sits in meditation.

Better than a hundred years
without wisdom and control
is a single day
in the life of one who is wise
and sits in meditation.

Better than a hundred years of living
in idleness and inactivity
is a single day
spent in intense effort.

Even if you live a hundred years,
unless you understand how
all things arise and pass away,
a single day in the life
of a person who understands

impermanence
is more valuable.

Even if you live a hundred years,
unless you perceive the deathless state,
a single day in the life of a person who sees
and understands
the deathless state
is more valuable.

Even if you live a hundred years,
unless you understand what is true,
a single day in the life of a person
who does understand
is more valuable.

Eating the Blame, 1

Everyone makes mistakes. Sometimes we lie. We don't mean to, but we do. Maybe we say we've completed something that we're planning to do. Maybe we report a situation and stretch its facts to meet our fantasy of what we'd like that situation to be, what our magic wand would make it. In a recent survey of forty thousand adults in the United States, 93 percent admitted to lying regularly and habitually, in spite of the personal costs that showed up in the form of stress, anxiety, deteriorating relationships, and worse.

We all make mistakes. Given the busyness of our lives, we forget to do things, to double-check. Or just plain don't have time to make good on a promise.

At a Buddhist temple it's easy to make mistakes. Especially your first few times walking in the door. There aren't a lot of clues about protocol. As a result, walking into a meditation hall can be like marching in a parade of errors.

It took me years to realize that a huge part of the Zen Buddhist tradition is about the teaching of humility. Without it, enlightenment can't happen. People may have experiences of sweet spaciousness, but so what? Without the compassion that grows out of our own experiences of humility, such breakthroughs can lead to Zen pride. It's downright dangerous.

So we *need* to make mistakes. Public ones are especially helpful. We need to hear ourselves tell a lie so that we can say, "I'm sorry," and correct ourselves. We need to step on the cushion or set up the altar incorrectly or forget to bow for the same reason: so that we can apologize. These are the actions that protect us from maniacal fantasies of perfection, a huge hindrance to spiritual growth.

> "Though a thousand verses
> of useless words may be offered,
> better is a single verse that,
> heard,
> brings peace."

"I'm sorry" fits the bill. At our temple we try hard to "eat all blame"—that is, to take as much personal responsibility for the problems and conflicts that arise as we can. Eating all blame is a learned behavior—and not an easy one if, like me, you were raised by a parent who smacked the bejesus out of you if you admitted fault. Likewise, admitting that you've lied isn't easy when you're living with someone who will commit the lie to memory and bring it up every time you two argue—from now until your last interaction.

And yet—we must.

I can tell how difficult Still Point seminary will be for someone by how easily the words "I'm sorry" come out of her mouth. Students who can't apologize eventually leave. They leave because they can't bear to look at their own human failings. Instead, they focus on mine. Since I have countless imperfections, starting with impatience and ending with talking with food in my mouth, I offer plenty of jumping-off points.

Unfortunately, focusing on someone *else*'s failings is generally an excuse not to look at one's own struggles. In other words, a waste of time.

> "Self-conquest is a far greater victory
> than conquering others.
> No one, not even a demon,
> can win back the victory
> of such a person.
> He is self-subdued.
> She lives in continuous restraint."

Twice now I've worked with wonderful people who wanted to be in the seminary but just couldn't make it work. In each case the hindrance was a deep inability to see or admit to their own shortcomings.

I watch the dharma students, cringing when I hear excuses for mistakes or just plain laziness. I try not to react when someone who has clearly made an error that resulted in a problem tells me all the extraneous reasons why the problem happened. There's so much in our every interaction—a lifetime of learned defensiveness, a lifetime of needing to be perfect. How have we done this to ourselves and our children?

I'm sorry.

One of the senior students is an older man, a veterinarian. Kogam has Frank Sinatra's blue eyes and the smile of a bodhisattva, a Buddhist saint. He's strong and specific, likes structure, and is determined to be a skillful dharma teacher. Strong-willed and sure of himself, Kogam doesn't suffer fools gladly. I worried about him at first. How would he get enough tastes of humility to protect him?

I had my answer when a big mistake was made by another dharma student—a student sincere but unmindful. The blunder followed a series of little mistakes—misplaced altar cloths, shoes casually kicked off at the door of the meditation hall where they caused people to trip. I watched Kogam's face as we figured out how to correct what had been done incorrectly. Although he wasn't as angry as I was, I'm guessing he was close. Didn't say a word, though.

A half-hour later, a knock on the office door. "P'arang, I'm sorry."

It was Kogam. He said he'd judged the other student and felt bad about it. I was happy for him because, in that moment, I knew that he had the humility it takes to cross the threshold of real awakening. An animal-healing Buddha. How did Detroit get so lucky?

> "Even if you live a hundred years,
> unless you understand what is true,
> a single day in the life of a person
> who does understand
> is more valuable."

EVIL
Quickly do good.
Protect your mind.
The mind of one who is slow in
doing good
will give in to mischief.

If you commit an evil deed
do not do it again.
Avoid finding pleasures this way.
In the end there will be
only misery.

If you perform good deeds
do them again and again.
Here is where pleasure lies—
and bliss.

An evil person may experience
happiness until the evil deed plays out,
but when it does
she will experience pain.

A person performing good deeds
may still meet with suffering
until his good deed bears fruit.
But when it does
there will be benefit.

Do not make light of harmful actions
thinking,
"It won't circle back to me."
Water falling drop by drop
will fill the largest pot.
Likewise a fool who commits
herself to harmful actions
is gradually filled with evil.

Do not underestimate good deeds
thinking,
"They won't circle back to me."
Water falling drop by drop
will fill the largest pot.
Likewise a person who performs good deeds
becomes goodness itself.

In the same way
that an executive with great wealth
and few bodyguards
avoids a dangerous place
one should avoid evil.
Avoid it
the way a person wanting to live
avoids poison.

If a person's hand is free
of wounds

he can carry poison
without being harmed.
In the same way the pure
come to no harm.

Whoever harms the harmless,
the pure and innocent,
will discover that evil
comes back at him
like a fine dust thrown
against the wind.

Evildoers are reborn
in miserable states.
Those who do good are
reborn in happy states.
Those who are free
from all clinging and craving
go on to perfect peace.

Not in the sky,
not in the ocean,
not in a mountain cave.
There is no place on earth
where you can hide from the
consequences
of an evil deed.

Not in the sky,
not in the ocean,
not in a mountain cave.
There is no place on earth
where you can hide
from your own dying.

Only Do Good

"If you perform good deeds
do them again and again.
Here is where pleasure lies—
and bliss."

One of the teaching methods Buddha used to convince people to take their practice seriously was to verbally create the vision of a perfectly beautiful young woman who would then age, die, and decay in a matter of minutes right before their eyes. Sometimes he had the monks and nuns who studied with him observe the decay of actual dead bodies. Both practices were pretty effective reminders that life is short; better not waste it.

One well-known Buddha story in this category is about a young courtesan, Sirima. Every day she offered delicious and plentiful food to the monks when they visited her street during their alms rounds. After a particularly generous day, one of the monks commented on Sirima's beauty when he returned to the monastery. A young monk who generally stayed behind now fell in love with her sight unseen, hearing the description of her. The next day he went on the alms round with the other monks so that he could see her for himself. Unfortunately, Sirima was too sick that day to serve them. Just when the monk had concluded that he'd missed out on seeing her, she walked through the room. He was a goner: she was the Juliet to his Romeo.

That night she died. When Buddha heard of her death he told the king to take her body to the cemetery but not to bury it. By the fourth day her body was bloated and covered with maggots. Buddha took all of his followers to see her. A woman for whom men would pay a thousand pieces of gold was now worth nothing. He couldn't give her away.

Seeing her, the monks were motivated to deepen their effort.

These days cities offer similar reminders that life is all too short. Maybe once a month I'll come across a body that I can't be sure is still breathing. The homeless population of Detroit doesn't feel greater than that of other major cities, but it feels more *visible* somehow. On some days there's a person on just about every corner in our neighborhood. They ask for money but are willing to take food. Mostly they're men, middle-aged. Two women are often found among them, however. One is thin, straggly-haired, crack-driven. The other, one leg missing, is in a wheelchair. She always asks for money for her kids.

The combination of alcohol, drug abuse, and a disinterest in shelters means that people openly eat, sleep, and sometimes die on the streets. So we see bodies a lot in our corner of Detroit. Most of the time it's clear that the person is sleeping something off. Sometimes, though, it isn't. In those situations, leaning down to watch for signs of breathing is scary. The person could haul off and whack you a good one. It's much easier to just walk away or ignore the body, telling yourself, "He's okay," or, "She's just drunk."

In our neighborhood it's generally the elderly women who have the courage to find out if someone is still breathing. They usually shout at someone else to check, though—and we do. Two weeks ago when I was walking into Comerica Bank on Woodward Avenue in the heart of downtown, a man was sprawled out on the concrete. Young. Dressed in clean clothes. People were walking past, ignoring him, even though it was freezing cold and he had no hat, no gloves or mittens, and only an open light jacket. An elderly woman—I'm guessing eighty—and I spotted him at the same time.

"Call the police." She wasn't asking; she was telling.

I leaned over the man and checked for breath signs but couldn't see any. Just then a bank security guard appeared and knelt down to shake the young man. He stirred a little. The old woman just looked at me and walked away.

Charnel grounds are everywhere.

Last week Catherine, one of the abbey residents, walked in the door and said, "Our sign just saved someone's life." We have a four-sided birch peace pole just outside the front door, as I mentioned earlier. It stands eight feet tall. Bright red four-inch carved letters form words of encouragement on each side. If you're standing at the front door of the abbey you see, "Pay attention!" and "Just this moment!" If you're standing on the sidewalk just beyond the yard, you see, "Do no harm!" and "Only do good!"

The pole is right next to the bus stop. It keeps people company and reminds us that there's always something we can do to be helpful, even if it's simply paying attention to what we're doing. That phrase alone—"Pay attention!"—would have saved a kitchen's worth of burned pots in my lifetime. I could see how the sign might spur people to consider how they're living out their lives, but *save* a life? I couldn't see the connection.

"Cat, what are you talking about?"

Usually Catherine is one of the sanest people around. But it was exam week for her, and we don't sleep a lot around here even under normal circumstances.

She told me that she'd said hi to a woman standing near the bus stop. The young woman had responded by asking her if she'd seen the body lying off to the side of Trumbull, several blocks south of the abbey. Cat hadn't. The woman explained that she'd been walking to Wayne State, rushing to get there in time to take an exam. She'd seen a female body but had kept walking, unwilling to be delayed. Just a few moments later, stopped at a light near the abbey and waiting to cross the street, she'd seen our pole.

"Only do good," it had urged.

She'd stared at it for a minute. She'd thought about Trumbull: it doesn't get a lot of foot traffic, and with four lanes and people driving fast, cutting from the river to various highways, it wasn't likely that someone else would see the body any time soon. Then she'd pulled out her cell phone to call 911.

When the woman had finished telling her story, Cat said, "Let's go check on her." They ran down to the woman, who by then was literally foaming at the mouth, in the throes of a seizure. By then a police car was coming down Trumbull, and Cat flagged it down. The police officers seemed confident that they could keep the woman alive until the ambulance arrived.

Cat walked the young woman back to our corner and offered to drive her to campus, since she was now late for her exam.

"No thanks," the woman said, going on her way.

After listening to the story, I asked Cat to say more about the young woman. She'd been about thirty, Cat estimated, and she'd been slim and wearing glasses. "You know, P'arang," Cat added, "when she walked away I could tell she was really happy that she'd done something—that she'd helped."

We think we can't be heroes, and then we are. Smack in the middle of an ordinary day.

Cat and her new acquaintance saved that woman's life by being quick to do good. Not hard to do, really. Pass the word.

CRUELTY
Everyone fears being hurt.
All of us fear death.
Knowing this,
see others as yourself
and cause no harm.

Everyone fears being hurt.
Life is dear to all of us.
Knowing this,
see others as yourself
and cause no harm.

A person seeking happiness
who strikes others
will find no happiness.

A person seeking happiness
who protects others
also seeking happiness
will find happiness after death.

Do not use harsh words.
They backfire.

Angry words breed trouble.
You will receive blow for blow.

Like a broken gong,
be still.
Know the stillness of awakening
where there is no anger.

Like a shepherd with a staff
who drives cows to pasture,
old age and death drive each of us.

Fools committing mischief do not see
the suffering
their deeds bring to themselves.
This suffering is as certain
as the pain
caused by fire.

A person who harms the harmless
or hurts the innocent
will experience the ten calamities:
torment; illness; injury; pain;
madness; danger from the government;
unfair accusations;
the loss of loved ones
and of wealth;
destruction of her house by fire;
and—after death—
she will be reborn in hell.

Even if you do penance,
even if you fast,
sleep on the ground,

and sit unmoving,
if you are not free of doubt
you will not attain peace.

He who—though richly adorned—
lives with self-restraint,
who is peaceful and virtuous,
who does not harm or hurt
or blame—
he is pure.

Rarely in this world
can one find
a person restrained by modesty,
a person who avoids reproach,
constantly.

Like a well-trained horse who,
when barely touched,
moves forward with energy and power,
be strenuous.
With your confidence and virtue,
with your effort and concentration,
with your investigation of the Dharma,
with your willingness to see yourself,
to act with restraint,
and heedfully,
you will free yourself of suffering.

As farmers channel water to their fields
and carpenters shape their wood,
so the virtuous
fashion themselves.

Becoming Goodness

Buzz cut. Biggest blue eyes I've ever seen—*beautiful* eyes. I can't guess her age. Twenty-four, maybe? She stands at the abbey door waiting for me to let her in. Her name is Elizabeth. Liz. She's trying to hold a two-year-old fireball in her arms. Paige. White-blond hair—pixie cut—and the same blue eyes. A rosebud mouth. She squirms out of her mother's arms and runs through the door as soon as the opening is wide enough.

They're in trouble.

> "Everyone fears being hurt.
> All of us fear death.
> Knowing this,
> see others as yourself
> and cause no harm."

I invite them in, feed them. Liz tells me that she learned about Still Point from a friend. It would be quiet and safe, the friend had said. Peaceful. Then she tells me her heart-wrenching story.

As she starts to talk I realize that she didn't really mean to say anything. The words just spilled out. Since she's too big for me to hold on my lap and rock, I start talking about resources in Detroit, places where they can spend the night, places where they can be safe. I want to say, "Stay at the abbey," but it would be too hard for Paige. In the back of my mind I tell myself I'll figure out something if they can't find a place. Maybe the basement would work. The abbey residents are patient and kind, and they'd say okay if I asked them. My friend Sansae is with me when Liz and Paige arrive. She has the same reaction: "We have to do something."

After lunch Liz heads out with her daughter and disappears, is untraceable for over a month. I try not to think she's dead. I try not to think about Paige. I do, though, almost all the time.

Then they show up at the abbey again. This time I have some money to give them to help her move. My board is generous, even though we don't have much ourselves. Liz goes to live with her mother. She starts coming to Sunday services. Then she comes to weekday sittings.

Slowly more details of her story come out. They're harsh, as Detroit can be sometimes. All she's known is abuse, she tells me as we share a cup of tea one afternoon. Her father should have died from his addiction to crack years ago, but somehow he didn't. He lived on to continue his indescribable cruelty toward his daughter. I can't believe Liz is sitting in the abbey kitchen, given all she's been through.

Not only has she brought some food this visit, but she also has one of my favorite magazines, *Adbusters,* under her arm. Her life is settling a little, she tells me. Her meditation practice is kicking in; she's starting to see how precious she is.

She hasn't seen her father in years. Decides it's time to track him down. She finds him on the street, not far from where she lives. More than anything in the world he wants to see Paige.

No.

Liz will visit him alone. She can hold her own. But the damage he's done is too deep, too painful, for her to trust him with Paige. "He likes kids too much," she says.

The next thing we know Liz's father is in the hospital. Maybe he's dying, even though he's still young. The drugs are doing him in. Liz decides to go see him even though the rest of her family begs her not to go. "It will be too awful," they tell her.

When she gets to the hospital he's gone. He's signed himself out and is back living on the street somewhere.

A week later Liz shows up at the abbey with enough food for a dozen people. She's made us a spicy zucchini and eggplant rice dish, along with eggplant and zucchini pancakes. Korean style. A huge salad. Cookies and chocolate, crackers and granola. She's been up since dawn preparing everything. Made her cousin Dee Dee go to the grocery store with her at seven A.M. to get ingredients. Then she cooked for four hours.

We can't eat the meal fast enough. It's unbelievably delicious. Best of all, there's enough left over for dinner and maybe even the next day's lunch.

I look at Liz after we finish eating. She's grinning from ear to ear, a happy angel. There's a visible halo over her head. I know you think I'm kidding, but I'm not.

11

OLD AGE
How can there be laughter?
How can there be joy when the world is ablaze
with craving and clinging?
Laughter and joy are
hidden by the darkness
of ignorance. When we realize
this truth, the wise among us seek
enlightenment.

You can just look
at a beautiful person
who has died—
now a heap of bones—
and see that nothing lasts.
Nothing.

The body wears out,
a nest of disease.
Fragile,
disintegrating,
dying.

Like gourds
discarded at the end of summer
are these bones.
What pleasure is there
in looking at them?

Bones are simply
a frame for our body.
Flesh and blood are the glue that
holds them together.
Inside?
Conceit, hypocrisy, decay, and death.

Everything man-made
wears out.
So do our bodies.
But the Dharma does not change.
Shining truth and lovingkindness live on
while virtue builds virtue.

The ignorant grow like oxen.
Their muscles grow
but their wisdom does not.
How many lives,
how many rounds
of rebirth
have I experienced without finding
the builder of this body,
this house of suffering?
Sorrowful it is to be born again
and again.

But, spiritual practice matured,
you will build no more houses for me, builder!
The rafters of ignorance are broken,
the main posts shattered.
The fever of craving is past.
My mind has attained the unconditioned.

Those who do not lead a spiritual life
in their youth
will look back with regret
in their old age,
pining away
like herons beside a fishless pond.

Not having attained the higher life
of the seeker,
they will lie like spent arrows
that have missed their mark,
bewailing a misspent past.

Staying Upright

Twice a year we teach a class called "A Buddhist Approach to Death and Dying." We start out with an exercise in which participants write about what a "good dying" would be for them. In the scenarios created we're typically all pain-free and filled with a deep sense of joy. Some of us have music playing; most of us are holding hands with someone we love. Rooms are darkened and incense is burning (or at least the room smells good). For Cat, a good dying would be to go during sex. Her second choice would be to die while pulling toast out of a toaster during an electrical storm. For Art, dying in his sleep works. Sudden is good for most people, and (outside of Art) most people want to be conscious. Generally people are divided over whether or not they want family members nearby.

Following the writing exercise, we talk in the class about the dying process, how there are emotional stages people go through—denial, rage, bargaining, depression, and finally acceptance. We review the physical stages as well—the loss of one's senses and bodily strength, memory loss, shifts in breathing patterns, and finally (usually after everyone else thinks the person is dead) the cessation of inner respiration.

At that point in the seminar everyone needs a break. People walk quickly out of the room, heading for the bathroom, for water, for caffeine, for chocolate—reminders that we're still very much alive, each of us. The training continues with teachings about dying—mostly that we die as we live, which means that spiritual practice matters *right now*. We talk about Buddha's teaching that there is no permanent soul, and we discuss how, after death, we'll move through specific bardos (or stages), each marked by particular characteristics, before we're faced with a new life (as a person, one hopes, and not as a worm or a ghost or worse!). We read excerpts from the Tibetan Book of the Dead. The discussion is always lively.

The training finishes with a conversation about how we can prepare for our own death, which could happen anytime, and how we can help others through their dying. We can, for instance, help relax any tension in the room. We can be the ones who tell the truth, who listen, who remember not to take anything personally. We can "just say no" to preaching and rescuing and make it clear to the dying person that we're okay with her dying.

Easy to say.

Hard to do.

One of my best friends in the whole world was Elsie Archer. I never thought of her as old, although her hair was definitely gray-white and her face was plenty wrinkled when I met her. We became friends at the Ann Arbor Zen Buddhist Temple, where we both volunteered. I admired her T-shirts and her stories about working with troubled teens in Detroit. I admired her gumption. She would correct the temple priest, something the rest of us never quite had the guts to do. At least not like Elsie. She was blunt. Pointed. Matter-of-fact. She was also fun and funny. She was my favorite Art Institute cruising companion. I loved her stories so much that I talked her into agreeing to co-write a book with me on aging the Buddhist way—just so I'd have an excuse to visit her.

But then she got sick.

It's sudden. Within a couple of weeks I'm driving north to Birmingham to visit her in a nursing home. My Elsie of hiking boots, khakis, and T-shirts is lying in a room surrounded by hospital machines and medicines. By the end of her second week there she knows the histories of all the staff, and they (along with the rest of us) adore her. A few days later, when I call to see how long the visiting hours last, I'm told she's been taken to the hospital. Kidney failure. She makes it back to the nursing home for another week or so, but then problems surface again. Back to the hospital. This time she doesn't come out.

I've been with dying people before. But this time I'm with one of my good friends. It's different. Way harder. I know I'm supposed to be calm, to listen, to joke, but when I reach her door, Elsie is literally withering away before my eyes. It's all I can do not to faint from the sheer emotion of that realization.

She looks at me.

"I'm dying, P'arang. It's okay. Everybody does, you know."

All right. I can breathe again. It's good old Elsie, helping me help her. Sitting in the chair next to her bed, I ask how I can be useful.

"Chant the Great Compassion Dharani. Then talk me through the bardos." Chanting fills the room.

> "Sin-myo jang-gu Tae-da-ra-ni
> na-mo-ra da-na-da-ra ya-ya
> na-mag-al-yak pa-ro-gi-je-se-ba-ra-ya
> mo-ji-sa-d-ba-ya
> ma-ha-sa-da-ba-ya
> ma-ha-ga-ro-ni-ga-ya. . . ."

Sometimes I stop to blow my nose or get some apple juice for Elsie, but mostly I chant and chant and chant. Three times I stop to read about the bardos, preparing her for the stages she'll go through after she dies and before a new birth.

By the time I go to see Elsie in the hospital the second time, her full circle of friends has kicked in. We're on a twenty-four-hour schedule so that she won't be alone. It's six A.M., and I'm taking over from Haju Sunim, the Ann Arbor temple's priest. Haju has been with her all night.

By this point Elsie can barely talk. But her practice is strong. I can feel it. All those years of meditation are serving her well. Suddenly her eyes open. She stares at me.

"I'm not scared, P'arang."

"Good. Then I'm not either."

I chant my heart out, knowing that her time is close.

> "Om sal-ba ba-ye-su da-ra-na
> ga-ra-ya da-sa-myong
> na-mak-ha-ri-da-ba. . . ."

The next afternoon Koho and I return to chant and read for Elsie. By this point she's in a coma, and I'm sure each breath will be her last one. But she keeps breathing in again, breathing in again. Koho and I just stay put, right there with her dying.

She goes peacefully the next day.

I miss her still and I thank her forever. Elsie showed me how to stay upright in the face of death and dying.

12

SELF
If you love yourself
you will guard yourself well.
Day and night
the wise guard themselves.

Establish yourself as a sincere,
spiritual seeker
and thus be free
from useless pain.
Then you can teach others.

Mold yourself
in accordance with the precepts.
Allow no gap in credibility,
no disgrace.

You are your own savior.
What other savior could there be?
When the savior and the saved
are one,
your work
is done.

In the same way that a diamond
can grind all other gems,
evil committed by a fool
crushes
the doer.

Like a vine strangling a tree,
a person's unwholesome actions
strangle her,
to the delight of her enemy.

It is so easy to do the things
that harm us—
and so hard to do the things
that don't.

Foolish people cling
to wrong views. They mock
the teachings of the enlightened ones.
And then they
reap what they sow.
Like a plant that dies when
it bears fruit,
foolish people bear the fruit
of their own destruction.

We create our own evil, you and I.
We defile ourselves.
We are the only ones
who can abandon our
evil doings.
We are the only ones

who can
make ourselves
pure.

Your purity
and
your impurity
depend on you.
Completely.
This is not
someone else's work.

Do not neglect your own spiritual efforts
for the sake of others' welfare,
even when there is need.
Instead, find your own
spiritual path
and then, seeing it clearly,
follow it with earnestness.

Collages

In the years before I fell into the arms of Zen I was a management consultant, primarily to Midwest-based companies. My claim to fame was strategic planning with an eye toward marketing and user-friendliness. In that capacity every fall for five years I drove to northern Michigan for the annual planning retreat of a favorite client. This was a multimillion-dollar human service agency run by a woman determined to do right by her staff—a difficult task even in upbeat financial times, given the industry's extremely low profit margins. Each year the president would ask me to show up with an entertaining activity for the middle of the retreat. One year, for example, we organized a scavenger hunt in which all the clues had something to do with leadership. Another year we crafted a group storyboard, sketching out the firm's most likely future.

Then I discovered collages.

Collages are big, multipictured posterboards, like the ones kids make for grade-school science projects. When collages are used in a visioning exercise, people are given a topic—say, "What I want my future to look like"—and then spend an hour and a half skimming through a pile of recycled magazines, ripping out pictures and words that strike them as being a part of their vision. Gluing the collection of images and words onto the board, individuals get to see how they really feel about the topic. The exercise is actually great fun.

When I introduced the idea to my client as a retreat option, she hesitated at first, then agreed to try it once to see what happened. Each staff member created a collage that portrayed that person's vision of the company. People were both surprised and happy to see that they shared the same hopes: profit in an exciting, compassionate, and ethical company. Since then, collages have become an institutionalized activity for the annual retreats.

I'd like to say that I came up with the idea of collages in a moment of sheer genius, but that's not what happened. It surfaced in a business-magazine article about advertising. The article's topic? "Why women wear stockings." As I recall, focus groups and surveys just couldn't answer that pressing question. Women kept reporting that they didn't *like* stockings. Period. On the other hand, they kept wearing them. Finally a researcher at MIT suggested trying a form of collage-making with groups of women.

The answer was immediate. When we choose to wear stockings, we do so because they make us feel sexy. Advertisers had a field day. Sexily stockinged legs showed up everywhere—in print, on television. I can still close my eyes and see a stockinged leg coming out of a limousine in a commercial that must be ten years old by now.

We live in a society driven by advertising. We're told to drink coffee; stay sexy; consume perfect, colorful martinis. Even though none of these things is spiritually helpful, it's excruciatingly hard to break free of the messages.

And yet that's our work.

At Still Point the precepts are the core tools we use to protect ourselves from getting too drawn into the world of advertising.

Each year between twenty and thirty people come forward to take the precepts in front of a roomful of witnesses. They've prepared for the moment by doing at least three thousand prostrations, chanting daily from the time they decide to take the precepts, and seriously reflecting on how they live each day. At the ceremony, each person commits to using the precepts as the principles by which they will live their lives. Watching, I always tear up. Partly it's out of gratitude for the precept-takers' commitment to living a deeply moral life. Partly it's because they've just committed themselves to seeing their lives clearly through a precept-colored lens.

For most of us this is not a pretty sight. We have a hard time telling the truth. We take things that haven't been given to us—someone else's time, office supplies, food we won't eat. We fog up our minds with drugs, alcohol, caffeine, television, the internet. (I'm so addicted to the internet that I make myself drive forty-five miles away to log on. If it were any more accessible to me, I'd be lost forever in the land of search engines. The net is just too perfect a drug for this information junkie.)

> "If you love yourself
> you will guard yourself well.
> Day and night
> the wise guard themselves."

Precepts force us to see how we're spending our time and what impacts us. Our spiritual practice deepens as a result. Mostly this is good news. On the other hand, as we live out the precepts it becomes increasingly difficult to lie about how well we take care of ourselves. We can't pretend we gave up coffee and yet still drink it on the sly (something I, for one, used to do).

We have to admit to ourselves that we're drinking more than one martini even though we've had the same glass in our hand all night. Once the precepts start taking up space in our brain, they become an alarm system that refuses to be silenced.

There's an old Zen story about an enlightened Zen master who would sit in meditation every night. About halfway through his sitting, he would shout at himself, "Don't let them fool you!" Then he'd shout, "No, master!" It was his way of protecting himself from the addictions and the advertising messages. It was his reminder to stay upright. It was his communication with himself: by shouting to his own mind, "You can't fool me anymore!" he was acknowledging that he was the one responsible for his own purity or impurity.

We are each responsible for ourselves, with our lives serving as a form of collage, giving us clues about where we need to focus our spiritual effort, where we need to just let go, and where we need to devote more energy. If we look with care, our lives tell us where we're harming others and where we're being clearheaded. The collage of our life also spotlights where we're being fooled (and reveals how we can trust ourselves more so that we won't be fooled anymore).

Like the Zen master, we're opening up to our own lives at Still Point, determined not to be fooled by ourselves—or anything else, for that matter. Painstaking work, if you can get it. But we're up to it somehow; we're a pretty fearless group, all things considered. Already several people have come forward to acknowledge drug and/or alcohol addictions, and we're starting a twelve-step program. Weight is being lost, televisions are getting turned off more often, and I have more and more company when I head out to pick up garbage on the street. And today? Today, I'm just drinking tea.

13

THE WORLD
Do not live for pleasure—
careless,
deluded.
Do not seek repeated births!

Pay attention to
everything.
Be meticulous.
People who are heedful
in this way are happy
in this lifetime and beyond.

Follow the path
of wisdom.
Do not tread where there is evil.
If you can live
on the earth in this way,
death will pass you by.

This world seems
heavenly

when it is really
a trap
for fools—
a bubble, a mirage.
Those who understand this
are liberated.

A person who used to be
lazy and ignorant
but now lives heedfully
lights up the whole world—
just like the moon
freed from a cloud.

Whoever dispels negative karma
through sincere spiritual effort
lights up the world indeed.
He is the moon coming out
from behind the clouds.

The few who understand what is real,
like the handful of birds able to
escape
a trapper's net,
fly to the heavens.

Swans fly
in the path of the sun.
In the same way
holy ones rise to the heavens
when they leave this world.

They have conquered
temptation and illusion.

Scorning the world hereafter
and violating the law of truth—
there are no limits to the damage
caused by a person's mischief.

A fool makes fun of generosity.
A mean person cannot enter heaven.
The wise rejoice in giving.
Happiness is their reward.

Better than ruling the world,
better than going to heaven,
better than being lord
of all existing realms is the fruit
of the sincere spiritual seeker's efforts.

Regarding Just This

"Whoever dispels negative karma
through sincere spiritual effort
lights up the world indeed.
He is the moon coming out
from behind the clouds."

The first time I saw him I thought he was one of the kids at Peace Camp. Every summer the Ann Arbor Zen Buddhist Temple sponsors a five-day camp at a local lake. Though ostensibly a camp for children, the chanting, meditation, arts and crafts, and campfires attract just as many adults as kids—sometimes more. Filled with fresh summer-morning energy after early sitting practice, people do a lot of running around and chasing each other. Watching the kids race around, I wondered who the tall one was.

Koho.

Only he wasn't a kid. He was a dark-haired, lanky twenty-year-old. Grinning through wire-rimmed glasses, he made the rest of us laugh until our stomachs ached. And yet when I first saw him meditate, I understood the expression "like a fish in water." He was a natural.

Years later, when I realized that I was headed for Detroit to start Still Point, I asked him what he thought.

"I'll go with you."

Koho was Still Point's second seminary student and first member of the board. He coached and consoled me through a poignant first year, even while facing his own dragons head-on. Hearing a rumor that he sometimes writes, I asked him if he would write a poem for our first holiday season card. He gave me this:

REGARDING JUST THIS
Lone leaves dance down Forest

Avenue past gray robes lapping up litter—
the river south of here
    into fractured concrete Belle Isle shore
    where last year   Drepung monks prayed standing before
    someone's millennium   sand of Yamantaka mandala

—whose bed became buildings
                this river—

Gray squirrel searches
for buried nuts and those not found
sprout to trees before long

All the world is Nansen's cat, this
    city of caves old
    Bodhidharma staring through vaulted walls
        in Michigan Central
Rail,

the effort of ferns up through
cracks in the station

platform, a joy: I could become

what I am

Cass Corridor
12 November 2000

Talent. The sangha quickly sensed an innate leadership as well. People started approaching Koho for advice about their practice. Crushes surfaced. Both men and women were drawn to him.

I started to worry. Would he get caught up in his popularity? He was starting to publish, and he was good. Would he become arrogant? Would he get lazy with his practice?

> "This world seems
> heavenly
> when it is really
> a trap
> for fools—"

At my most neurotic I was convinced that Koho would leave Still Point. We're a small pond. His is a bigger world. He went away for a few weeks after one of our best friends died. They'd been very close, and the death had been a painful surprise. I half-expected never to see him again. After all, he was newly married to the perfect woman and had a book to write.

By then it was clear that Detroit was going to be rough-and-tumble-filled. The problems of the big city were primal and complicated, and they were now ours. The rhythm of the parade of heartbreaks that would walk through our door was set.

Then one Sunday, arriving at the temple, I noticed how much attention had been put into the setting up of the meditation hall.

> "Pay attention to
> everything.
> Be meticulous.
> People who are heedful
> in this way are happy
> in this lifetime and beyond."

Setting up the room for a service requires painstaking mindfulness. In order to accommodate the fifty to sixty people who attend, mats and cushions need to be placed in specific places. The altar also needs attention: Buddha in the middle; water and incense bowls placed a couple of inches in front of him; two candles just in front, equidistant from Buddha and the edges of the tabletop.

Koho has always done a wonderful job setting up the hall. When he's the person responsible, I know everything will be in its rightful place. That Sunday, when I walked up to the altar to begin our morning chant, I was stopped cold. Everything was in its correct place. But there was more. Someone had taken the time to carefully make three circles in the ashes in the incense bowl, and the stick of incense stood straight up, exactly in the middle of all three.

Koho was back.

In that moment I knew that he would be okay, that he knew how to use heedfulness as a refuge. I knew that he would be a skillful dharma teacher and that he would be able to shrug off all of the fame and fortune determined to come his way. More important, I knew that he was ready to give this path everything he's got.

BUDDHA
Those whose conquest of desire
is complete
cannot be moved
by desire.
They create no karma.
For them there are
no entanglements,
no cravings for pleasure.

The wise,
intent on meditation,
delight in the peace that comes
from letting go.
Such mindful people
even the gods cherish.

Rare it is
to be born human.
More rare still
to hear the Dharma.
Most rare
to see a Buddha.

Shun evil.
Cultivate good.
Purify your heart.
This is the teaching of Buddha.

Patience that is enduring
is the best discipline.
One who practices such patience
with her whole heart,
letting go
of her addiction to desire,
harming no one,
oppressing no one—
Nirvana is hers.

Do not harm.
Do not insult.
Use the precepts to help yourself.
Eat modestly.
In solitude and intent on meditation
follow the teachings of Buddha.

Rain could turn
into coins of gold,
and we would still crave.
Sensual pleasures are sweet
and yet so painful.

Knowing this,
the student of Buddha refuses
to crave pleasure
even in the form of heaven.

Fear may lead a person to seek
refuge
in the mountains
or in the forest,
in groves of sacred trees
or temples.

But these refuges are not safe
because
they are not the final refuge.
The final refuge is the one taken in
Buddha, Dharma, and Sangha.

When we take that refuge,
we come to see the Four Noble Truths
of suffering, the cause of suffering,
the possibility of the release of suffering,
and the mechanics of that release—
the Noble Eightfold Path.

This is the supreme refuge.
By seeking refuge
in these three jewels one is freed
from all sorrow.

It is hard to find people
with great wisdom.
They are rare.
Happy is the family into which
one with wisdom is born.

Blessed is the birth of the Buddha.
Blessed is the teaching of the Dharma.
Blessed is the refuge in Sangha.
Blessed are those trained in these refuges.

Honor those who have
overcome wrong views
and rid themselves
of sorrow—
whether they are Buddha or his students.
The value of this reverence is
unimaginably beneficial.

Mr. Kung Buddha

"Rare it is
to be born human.
More rare still
to hear the Dharma.
Most rare
to see a Buddha."

An eye twitch drove me to meditation. Twice my eye doctor suggested that sitting practice would help me conquer the stress that was making the top of my face wiggle to its own song. Out of desperation I signed up for a six-week meditation course. I was clueless about Buddhism.

Within three weeks the eye twitch was gone. In between sittings, my meditation instructor, Haju Sunim, would talk about Buddhist principles or tell Buddhist stories. Each time I would sit there and say to myself, "That's what I think!" Having spent over eighteen years working my way through educational institutions, I couldn't believe that there could be a major spiritual tradition that I knew nothing about—especially a tradition that so closely aligned with my personal values that it was a little scary. But it was true.

There had to be a catch.

Perhaps it was a cult.

To find out, I decided to learn Chinese so that I could read the sutras in their original language. That way I could discover the secret punchline; I could get the real gist of the "Give us your firstborn or we'll kill you" sutra, or the "Give us all your money or you'll go to hell forever" sutra. To find a Chinese teacher I went to the University of Michigan intending to put a note requesting a tutor on one of the language studies bulletin boards. Instead I saw a small handwritten note: "Chinese teacher. Please call Mr. Teyen Kung." A phone number was listed below his name.

I called the number.

It turned out that Mr. Kung was an elderly Chinese gentleman with the energy of a teenager. His family had owned banks in China before the revolution took their assets away. Mr. Kung had been an engineer responsible for designing and building massive public works projects. The two of us agreed to meet weekly, during my lunch hour. Mr. Kung insisted on feeding me. Occasionally I would run errands for him. He refused to take any money, instead sending me home with food, books, and small gifts for my "very beautiful" daughter.

For two years we struggled through a basic Chinese workbook and a primary-school textbook. By that point it was clear to both of us that I would never understand Chinese well enough to read the sutras. A trip to China then demonstrated that I would never be able to speak comprehensible Chinese. As just one indicator, after weeks of saying what I thought was "Thank you very much" to hundreds of mainland Chinese, I was told by a young English-speaking tour guide that I was really saying, "Your baby is going to the toilet."

Fortunately, by that time I had grown to love and trust Mr. Kung, and we had discovered that we had Buddhism in common. I was inhaling Zen. Immersed in Pure Land Buddhism, he became my personal bodhisattva, always kind, always helpful. When I was ordained as a dharma teacher, I didn't know that families traditionally give something to the temple. Mr. Kung showed up after the ceremony with an ancient jade urn. Later, when I went on a pilgrimage to Korea, he gave me a hundred dollars to help with travel expenses.

When I told him about Still Point and said that I would be moving to Detroit, he sat quietly. Then a storm of questions erupted. "What about your daughter?" ("She's going to school in Wisconsin.") "What about house and car payments?" ("I'll have a stipend that will cover my monthly living expenses.")

Then, in September 2001, after I'd moved, the phone calls started. "When will you be in Ann Arbor? Come to my house!" And I would go.

Each time he had a gift for Still Point, although he has yet to visit the temple. The first gift was a big bag of wrist malas. I had told him that we needed to figure out how to help one of the seminary students to pay his tuition, so he sent these malas—I think there were thirty in the bag—for the young man to sell. Then he started giving me food for Detroit. We must have fifty pounds of dried beans by now; we can't give them away. He keeps us in rice and in canned vegetables too. Every once in a while he throws in a box of dry cereal for Cat, or biscuit mix. We have three cupboards full of instant mashed potatoes. He is Buddha.

Almost every Monday the telephone rings: "Geri, when can you come here?!" Twice he has filled my car with secondhand clothes—designer clothes from wealthy friends—with instructions to give them away. Once he filled the car with loaves of bread for the soup kitchen down the street. I could barely see over the mountain of cracked wheat and rye. Sometimes he gives me Buddhist books and CDs to give away to anyone who wants them.

We need protein, so he gave us five pounds of cheese one visit. Said he could get us more if we needed it.

At the end of our first year we were pretty low on cash to pay our expenses. I didn't say anything to Mr. Kung about it. He didn't ask. But he called me in the middle of one week. "Geri! When will you be in Ann Arbor?! Can you come before next Monday?" I made an excuse to go see him a couple of days early. When I arrived, he handed me an envelope and told me not to open it yet. Though curious, I waited until I got back to Detroit. In it was a check for a thousand dollars. I'm guessing it was all the money he had. He got us through the month. Mr. Kung Buddha.

C H A P T E R

15

HAPPINESS
Truly we are happy.
Others may hate.
We will not.
Even when surrounded by people who hate
we do not.

Truly we are happy.
Others are sick.
We are not.
Even when surrounded by sick people
we live free
from sickness.

Truly we are happy.
Others may wrestle with life.
We do not.
Surrounded by unhappy people
we live free
from struggle.

Truly we are happy.
Free of obstacles to happiness
we feed on joy.

Victory produces hostility,
because the ones who are defeated
live in grief.
Letting go of victory and defeat,
the tranquil mind lives
in happiness.

Desire is a fire without equal.
Hatred is the greatest evil.
There is no happiness greater than peace.

Hunger is the most difficult disease.
Conditioned things cause
the greatest suffering.
When we understand this
and can see clearly,
we grow spiritually.

Health is the highest prize,
contentment the greatest wealth.
A loyal friend is the best relative
and Nirvana is supreme peace.

When you taste the sweetness
of solitude
and tranquility
you become free
of sorrow and sin,
fully savoring the sweetness of
the way.

It is good to see the holy ones:
to live with them brings happiness.
Not spending time

with the unskillful
and unwise
also brings happiness.

Therefore, like the moon
following its ordained path,
let each one keep company
with people who are
wise, steadfast, loyal, and pure.

"Letting Go" Practice

Tanya walked in the door for a Wednesday evening sitting and announced that she was on day five of a thirty-day fast. She was only drinking juices. The rest of us were in awe of her gumption. How could she do that and still function?

She motivated several of us to do our own fasts. Normally we aren't a collection of people that includes fasters. Food is too important to us. Particularly at the abbey. After six A.M. prostrations, chanting, and sitting, we're hungry. At one P.M., after our noon sitting, we're hungry again. At night, more food.

On the other hand, watching Tanya I remembered a three-day energy fast I'd done a couple of years earlier. Compared to thirty days, three days would be a breeze. I decided to try it again. The pattern of the fast is simple: each morning you get to drink fruit juices—pineapple, papaya, mango. (Not orange juice, because it's too acidic.) From noon on it's green vegetable juices, followed by the juices of all the vegetables waiting in your refrigerator to be used: kale, broccoli, celery, onions, garlic. At the end of the day, blueberry juice is okay. This isn't a *diet* fast, only a *cleansing* one. You aren't supposed to get hungry.

I picked a Monday to start my three-day fast. Knowing what was facing me, I turned Sunday into a steady inhalation of junk food—sugar, caffeine, carbohydrates. Burt and Julie brought bagels to our post–morning service potluck, and I grabbed one from the top of the enormous pile, thinking it was pumpernickel. When it turned out to be chocolate, I ate the whole thing before going back to the pile for more. Delicious.

Day one, Monday morning, was a cinch. Denying yourself caffeine is no problem when you have yesterday's leftovers coursing through your system. I went for a walk with Haju in Ann Arbor. We talked about our kids, dharma, and the monk I mostly affectionately call Samu Sunim. Errands made the rest of the day fly. A trip to the printer for flyers. A visit to the food co-op for kale, tofu, fruit, and cheese. A run to the bank, and a quick stop at the library to see if there were any new art books on the shelves. I didn't even notice that I was only drinking vegetable juices, my chore list was so long. An evening bath promised an easy day two.

Wrong. I woke up worried about my children's future in a world ravaged by violence and pollution, and angry at myself for not taking better care of my body. Worse yet, I was hungry—*mean* hungry. The day went downhill from there. Hostility took over my system as though aliens had found a secret passageway into my thinking neurons. When I sat down at my desk at midmorning to work and instead discovered a virus munching away at my computer, I understood, finally, why people throw computers out of windows.

By noon I'd had it. The fast sucked and my life was a failure. I had wasted years on the wrong teacher. A big bowl of green vegetable broth gave me only enough energy to keep grousing. Poor, poor, pitiful me. On top of everything else, I told myself, society's a mess, racism is everywhere, the situation in the Middle East is getting worse, and we're all running out of oxygen to breathe.

I was too miserable even to cry. So I sat. For an hour I

watched the parade of self-centered whining prance through my brain. I could feel my body detoxing, but it didn't matter. Every negative thought stuck, and I didn't have the energy or willpower to let it go. When I couldn't bear it anymore, I went to bed.

Day three. A Wednesday. I had to wake up the other abbey residents with the Great Compassion Dharani. My tongue was pretty swollen with all of the sugar trying to escape my system. The chant came out fumbly and tenuous. "Seeng-myooo-ggg-jang-goooo Taeeee-duh-rah-niiii. . . ." When we did prostrations I totally lost count of where we were, getting back on track only when Ango just stopped getting up for the next one. After thirty minutes of meditation we got up to do Yebul, which is an ode of homage to the three jewels (Buddha, Dharma, Sangha) and the major bodhisattvas. It's a complicated chant, with rhythmic beats on the moktak at specific intervals, interspersed with prostrations. It took me over three years to learn how to lead it, even though the entire chant takes only a couple of minutes. That morning I was so dizzy I wasn't sure I'd make it through the chant without fainting or throwing up. I did—but just barely.

Just after I finished a breakfast of pineapple and mango juice, the phone rang. It was Arthur, calling from work. He wanted to know if I'd seen the lotus lanterns he'd left on the back porch for me. We had schemed to order some for Buddha's birthday, two weeks away. I had asked him to order big round paper and cardboard lanterns in pale pinks and whites. Lit up, they're pure beauty—a soft blanket of color that fills the meditation hall. I had been searching for a dozen or so. Art had found a Korean company on the internet that sold them, and I knew he'd ordered several dozen. Apparently they'd arrived.

Great! I set the phone down on the counter with Arthur in mid-sentence and rushed out to inspect the shipment. Instead of soft, delicate lanterns, what I saw when I opened the box was neon-pink plastic tubes. When they were unfolded, they looked like children's beach balls without tops or bottoms. Most had Korean words written all over them and a picture of baby Buddha on at least one side.

I hurried back to the phone and took a deep breath.

"Art, they're the wrong lanterns."

"I know."

"Can we return them to get our money back?"

"No."

A long pause. Finally, his voice again.

"I need to learn Korean."

We both started laughing. There wasn't anything to do but let go of our expectations, both of us. We laughed until we had sore stomachs. Suddenly I was happy again, remembering how powerful "letting go" practice really is. I was happy again, grateful that the juice fast had shown me how much letting go there is left to do. It is my life's work still. And forever.

16

TRANSIENT PLEASURES

Indulging in transient pleasures
while failing to do
the real work
of our lives
leads us to envy the ones who have
spent time and energy
on their spiritual work.

Let a man be free from clinging
to pleasure
and his aversion to pain,
for clinging to
pleasure creates sorrow.
And both pain and aversion to it create sorrow
    as well.

Sorrow arises out of pleasure.
So does fear.
So freeing yourself from clinging
to pleasure
will free you from fear and sorrow.

From passion spring grief
and fear.
Those who transcend passion's bonds
have no grief
or fear.

From sensuous delight come grief
and fear.
Those who transcend the bonds of
sensuous delight
have no grief
or fear.

From lust, grief.
From lust, fear.
Those who transcend
lust's bonds
have no grief
or fear.

Any kind of craving
causes grief and fear.
Let go of craving
to be free of both.

The woman who possesses
character,
insight,
wisdom, and
compassion,
who is just,

speaks the truth,
and focuses on her own work,
is a woman held dear
by the world.

The man in whom a desire
for enlightenment
has surfaced,
whose mind is driven to wake up,
whose thoughts are not
confused by sensuality—
this man is called *uddham-soto,*
"he who goes upstream."

Just as a person
who has been gone for a long time
is welcomed on his safe return home with joy
by his relatives,
friends,
and well-wishers,
so will you be welcomed,
when you move beyond this life,
by the good deeds you have done
in this lifetime.

Mojo

I look out the abbey window and see pale green grass making its way through the ground in the back yard. Dandelions are everywhere. In the front, clusters of red tulips surround the porch. They, in turn, are bordered by bright yellow daffodils. The lavender bush is starting to show its vivid color, and people are walking around without coats. It's only fifty degrees, but in Detroit fifty degrees is spring.

It's the season of love. The young people of the Still Point sangha start to pair up. First one couple gels. Then another. Phone calls to abbey residents double, then triple. The three young handsome, unattached male residents have been duly noticed. The race is on. I feel sorry for the young men and women who call. They don't know that they're part of a growing collective of people with crushes on abbey men. As for Cat, the young woman resident, her big green eyes and red hair turn grown men to mush. Even the electricians rewiring the rooms ask me to take messages to her from them.

A beautiful young woman notices one of the dharma students for the first time. I watch her fall in love with him before my very eyes. Before I know it, he's in love back. It's an exquisite dance. Other dharma students—the unmated ones—see each other in a new way, as potential partners.

Sparks fly all over the place.

"From sensuous delight come grief
and fear.
Those who transcend the bonds of
sensuous delight
have no grief
or fear."

I try not to worry about the lot of them. The half-life of being
in love is about six weeks. Then what will happen? Clearly there
will be broken hearts.

Just when I decide I'm imagining all the romance in the air, a
dear friend from Chicago comes for an overnight stay. "This
temple has great mojo," he tells me. When I ask the other residents later what he meant, they laugh out loud. "The word *mojo*
comes from New Orleans," Drew says. "It can have a sexual con-
notation—you know, *I've got my mojo working.*" Before I know it
we're chanting, "We're too sexy for our robes, too sexy for our
incense," and prancing around the place, taking a welcome
break from abbey formality.

The next day, three young men come to visit. They're martial
artists—a black belt, a blue belt, and their teacher. After two
hours at the abbey, the teacher says, "This place has great energy."

Cat looks at me and grins. "Mojo."

At the dharma student meeting we talk about love affairs and
how people fall in and out of love in sanghas. We're good
matches for each other in the sense that we have the same values
and the same "goal": spiritual growth. The main thing, we con-
clude in our discussion, is to be as upright as possible while we're
in a relationship. That way, if it doesn't last, each person will be
able to continue coming to the temple. I tell them, "It's important
to protect each other's practice."

They just look at me and grin. Knowing from my own experience the sorrow that grows out of the impermanence of pleasure, and knowing how the fear of losing a relationship leads to grasping and craving, I hurt for the heartbreaks that will inevitably come.

> "Sorrow arises out of pleasure.
> So does fear.
> So freeing yourself from clinging
> to pleasure
> will free you from fear and sorrow."

Suddenly I feel weary, unable to protect any of them. The Buddha statue sitting behind me tugs on my arm and whispers in my ear. "You be your own lamp and let them be theirs," he says. "Spring is just spring." I grin back at the sparkly eyed dharma students, resolving to buy extra chocolate for whoever shows up needing some. It should happen about mid-July, I reckon.

ANGER
Forsake anger.
Forsake pride.
Sorrow cannot touch a person
who has moved beyond
himself.

The person who
controls her anger,
reining it in as though
it were a runaway chariot,
is a true charioteer,
unlike those who
loosely hold on to the reins.

Overcome anger
with friendliness.
Overcome evil
with good deeds.
Overcome stinginess
with generosity.
Overcome lies
with truth.

Tell the truth.
Do not give in to anger.
Give what you can,
even if you own but a little.
These three steps will lead you
to the heavens.

People who do
no harm,
who are restrained
in their actions,
reach a state of Nirvana
where they no longer suffer.

If a person guards his behavior
day and night,
keeping his intentions pure,
hindrances will drop away.

There is an old saying:
"They blame the person who
is silent.
They blame the person who speaks often.
They even blame the person who says little."
No one is exempt from being blamed
for something.

In this world
there is not now,
there has never been,
nor will there ever be

a person who is always blamed
or always praised.

On the other hand,
a person who
lives a quiet and kind life
every day,
who is
intelligent,
wise,
and virtuous—
this person will be praised
by the wise.
Even the gods
praise such a person.

Be heedful of the role
your body plays in your life.
Give up the actions
that lead to sorrow.
Instead do the things
that lead to joy.

Be heedful of your speech.
Restrain it.
Watch out for angry words.
Trade them in for
virtuous ones.

Watch closely for anger
in your thinking:

restrain it;
then let it go.
Use your mind as
a tool for compassion and wisdom.
Always.
Do what you need to do
to keep your mind clear
and awake.

Pay attention to your intentions.
Control your body,
tongue,
and mind.
This is the restraint
of wisdom.

Eating the Blame, 2

I'm sitting in a metal chair in the third-floor hallway of the Oakland County Courthouse. The traffic on Telegraph Road is picking up; it's almost rush hour. This is hour three of waiting to be called as a character witness for a sangha member. Starting Still Point, it never occurred to me that the job description for dharma teacher would include going to court, but apparently it does. This is my sixth visit to a courtroom to play the role of witness to another person's uprightness. Several times I've attended to support a member who publicly identified a police officer known for harassing gay men. Other times I've spoken in support of parents trying to protect their children from violence.

Anger is everywhere. At the next courtroom door a young woman is so angry at her former partner that she can only sob in the arms of a best friend. Three feet away from me a middle-aged couple in identical royal blue outfits are arguing vehemently with a court official who won't help them get a court order to protect them from their own daughter.

"She's already threatened to kill us three times!" the woman cries.

"Once she actually tried," the husband adds.

The court official looks sympathetic but shakes his head.

"There's nothing I can do."

As they walk away disappointed, the woman says to the man, "She's going to kill us." He nods.

There is so much anger.

Living in the close quarters of an abbey, we all have to forgive each other's mistakes every day, since they happen all the time. Someone leaves a bundle of clothes in the dryer. The milk is used up without warning or replacement. Or the one I do best: we make plans for the building without letting everyone else know (like the time I invited an entire high-school class to visit when one of the residents needed quiet to study for finals). If we feed our flash of irritation at another resident it can quickly grow into anger. And yet if we get angry at each other, it's difficult to live together, to practice together. The whole building suffers.

So we clean up after each other. We fold laundry that isn't ours. We make a special run to the grocery store. We stay up late to do a second cleaning of the kitchen.

> "Tell the truth.
> Do not give in to anger.
> Give what you can,
> even if you own but a little.
> These three steps will lead you
> to the heavens."

When we realize we've made mistakes at the abbey, we apologize quickly and openly and then make amends as best we can. In fact, even if we aren't the one who made the mistake we make amends. It's called "eating the blame." This practice stops anger quickly because the emotion isn't given a chance to fester. Instead, its source is transformed.

The basement used to stink of cat spray from pets owned by

the previous tenants. I scrubbed the entire floor on my hands and knees with straight bleach. No change. Then Cat got a duckling that needed to spend time there growing a thicker pelt before he hit his new home, the back yard. The combination of duck poop and cat spray was pungent. My lavender atomizer couldn't begin to compete.

The smell was a constant minor irritation to all of us. In another house I'm guessing that there would have been at least one big argument about whose responsibility it was to fix the problem. Every once in a while, walking downstairs, I was just plain frustrated. "We can do better," I said to myself.

One day I asked Cat for ideas for solutions. She suggested that we get vinegar and scrub the floor with that. We cut a deal. She'd buy the vinegar and I'd scrub the floor. She'd also put some hay down for the duckling.

When I got home from court that day she'd already scrubbed the entire basement floor with vinegar. It probably took all afternoon. Instantly all of my irritation about the basement was transformed into gratitude for her effort. All of the tension I brought home from the courthouse was lifted. There's *good* in the world. Proof comes in the form of simple acts of eating the blame. I was so touched I baked a pizza for the abbey "just because," cleaning out the refrigerator while I was at it. Then I scrubbed the smelly compost bowl clean, chanting the whole time.

Later on, falling asleep, all I could think was how much that courthouse couple could use a Cat in their lives right about now.

IMPURITY
Before you know it you'll be like
a withered leaf
close to falling from the tree of life.
How have you prepared yourself for the journey?

Be your own island.
Work diligently.
Become wise.
Free of flaws and passions
you will enter the heavenly realms.

Your life is closing in on its end.
Death's presence is at your door.
There is no place to rest.
How have you prepared yourself for the journey?

Be your own island.
Do your spiritual work!
Become wise!
Free of flaws and passions
you will be free from the cycle of
birth and death.

The wise woman removes
her flaws
little by little,
one by one,
in the same way that a good silversmith
removes the impurities from silver.

Just as rust, once started,
corrodes iron,
unskillful deeds
and violations of moral law
destroy us slowly
but surely.
Not reciting scriptures
leads to rusty understanding.

Not taking care of our homes
leads to their falling apart.
Laziness destroys beauty
and heedlessness rots
our meditation.

Adultery destroys marriages
and greediness rusts generosity.
Bad qualities are stains that taint us,
not only in this world
but in the next one as well.

The worst stain
is ignorance.
Abandon this.
I beg you.

Life is so easy for someone
who has no shame,
who is as impudent as a crow,
who is a gossip,
vain, intrusive, and corrupt.

Life is hard
for people who quietly decide
to follow the Dharma
and seek purity.
Life is hard
for people who are cheerful
without bragging,
live cleanly,
and practice moderation.

The person who destroys
the lives of other people,
speaks falsehood,
takes what is
not offered,
commits adultery,
is addicted to drugs
or alcohol—
this person harms herself deeply.
She is digging up her own roots even now.

Remember this, friend:
People who have no control
over themselves
harm themselves and others.
Do not let anger, greed, and wickedness

drag you down with
their false promises.

People are generous
for different reasons
and in different ways.
Finding fault with someone else's
generosity
will only cause you to lose
your own peace of mind.

The ones who have given
up the habit
of finding faults in others
will know peace,
day and night.

There is no fire like desire,
no vice like hatred,
no trap like delusion,
no undertow like craving.

It is so easy to see others' faults,
and so hard to see our own.
We expose the flaws of others
quickly and easily
and then hide our own
like a person who cheats on a losing throw.

Those who look for others' faults
and are quick to take offense
only multiply their own wrongdoing.

Watching for others' faults only pushes us
farther and farther away from
the destruction of our own
impurities.

There are no footsteps in the sky,
and saints have no signs.
Yet most people want both footsteps and signs.
They delight in them.
Meanwhile, the enlightened ones transcend both.
No footsteps.
No signs.

A Rose Is a Rose

"The ones who have given
up the habit
of finding faults in others
will know peace,
day and night."

Last Sunday was Mother's Day. For the dharma talk I spoke about how we're *all* mothers. Some of us are mothers of children. Some of us are mothers of pets or plants. Some of us are mothers of computers or work teams or a building. Some of us are mothers of books, cars, and garbage cans. We're all caring for someone or something. We're all responsible.

Earlier in the week, thinking about how difficult it is to be a great mother, I wished that Still Point had enough money to buy a rose for everyone in the sangha, to thank people for their maternal leanings. Instead I bought a brick of cheese for the potluck that follows the service.

Walking out of the meditation hall after our last bows, I saw a huge bucket out of the corner of my right eye. It was filled with long-stemmed red roses. Recovering from my initial shock, I concluded that this must have been the work of Maurice. He has an uncanny ability to know what's needed in a moment. Sometimes he's ahead of the rest of us.

Maurice started coming to Still Point as soon as we opened. I thought he might be a journalist at first, because he often carried a little notebook with him. Tallish, thin, handsome, almost hunky. Mid-thirties maybe. Some part Asian, some part something else. His skin a soft gold that freckles.

Early on Maurice started doing kind things for Still Point. He framed a bodhi leaf so we could have at least one Buddhist picture for our empty little office. Even though our long retreats conflict with his work schedule and he can never attend, he always makes bottles of special sauces we can use on our stir-fry meals to make the cook's job easier at these busy times. He has taken our hundreds of random photographs and pieces of memorabilia and turned them into a wonderful Still Point album.

Every Sunday Maurice shows up with enough food for everyone who stays after the service—gourmet style. We try not to fight over it. When Still Point's first dharma student died, the sangha mourned him deeply. At the end of forty-nine days of services we decided to go to his favorite restaurant, Harmonie Gardens, to eat his favorite foods, smoke his favorite brand of cigarettes, and drink Turkish coffee in his name. When I went up to the restaurant counter to pay the bill, Maurice appeared beside me. He shoved a hundred dollars into my hand. "To help," he said.

Another time we organized a "dharma combat party" for Koho to help pay for his seminary fees. He had to sit at the front of the room and answer any question the thirty-plus people at the party asked him. Some people asked about spiritual practice, some about koans. Tough questions. How does he love? How does he hate? Why read the sutras? It was an energizing, moving, and often hilarious night. Koho was at his best. Maurice showed up for the event with over two dozen huge black-and-white photographs of Buddha and bodhisattva figures. He had matted each one. He gave them to Koho to sell as part of the fundraiser.

Here's the real clincher. In the last two years, we've all had good times and bad. There have been arguments, upsets, couples breaking up, family members going down the tube. You name it; it's happened. It's life. It's Detroit—a big city. Yet not once, in all the upheaval, have I heard Maurice say an unkind word. Not about a person. Not about an event. Instead he's continued to perform prescient kind acts. He regularly takes one of the paranoid schizophrenic members home on Sundays, for example—although none of us knew at first. (Since Daniel can get a little distracted, Maurice wanted to make certain he made it okay.) And when I spent an entire weekend on the receiving end of someone's vicious rage, Maurice was the one who hugged me after the Sunday service and said, "You're doing okay, P'arang." His kind words came just as I was starting to wonder what plane tickets to Australia cost these days. How did he know?

His energy is pure and his heart is unstoppable. Every week I catch him in moments of pure compassion. When he dies, the man is headed straight for Tusita heaven. Of that I'm certain.

THE JUST
The person who settles matters hastily
is not just.
A woman is wise only when
she first considers
what is right and what is wrong,
truthful and non-truthful,
peaceful and not peaceful,
before making a decision.

The wise man is not arbitrary.
He is impartial,
judging according to the law of the Dharma.
The just man guards Dharma
and abides by it.

Talking a lot
does not make us wise.
Being free of hate,
being fearless,
and refusing to do harm—
these make us wise.

A woman cannot be considered
well versed in the Dharma
just because she talks about it.
On the other hand,
a person who has never heard
the teachings of Buddha
but knows the truth of the Dharma
from her own experience
is well versed in the teachings.

Just because his head is gray
does not mean a man is necessarily wise.
Ripe in age
we are only old men.

One who is inoffensive,
virtuous,
honest,
self-restrained,
free of flaws—
this is a person who can be
honored.

Good looks
and a honeyed tongue
do not make a woman attractive
if she is—
at the same time—
jealous, deceitful, and selfish.

On the other hand,
the person who has refused

to give in
to envy, lying, and ego
is deeply attractive.

A shaven head does not
make a monk
if one is undisciplined,
tells lies,
is full of desire
and greed.
Who are you trying to kid?
A monk is the person
who has subdued
his unwholesome tendencies,
large and small.
This one is a monk
because evil has been
overcome.

Just because a man knows
how to use a begging bowl
does not make him a monk.
Only by leading a moral life
do we become holy.

And a woman is not wise
simply because she has taken
a vow of silence.
Awareness,
clarity,
and a willingness

to do the work to
choose wisely
make a sage.

Discernment.
Choosing good over evil.
With these
wisdom is uncovered.
If you harm others
you are not noble.
Noble ones do not hurt living beings.
Period.

Not through scholarly accomplishment,
not by simply keeping the precepts,
not by observing ritual,
not with the attainment of
meditative absorption,
not by solitude
is the bliss of wisdom found.
A wise person will not rest content
until all of her mind's defilements
have been uprooted.
This is wisdom.

Dharma Olympics

"A shaven head does not
make a monk
if one is undisciplined,
tells lies,
is full of desire
and greed.
Who are you trying to kid?"

In 1993 I attended the Parliament of World Religions in Chicago. It was a special honor, although I didn't realize it at the time. The last parliament was held a hundred years ago. Both were gatherings of religious leaders from almost every denomination. Even the Dalai Lama attended the 1993 event, I think, though the pope sent his regrets. Native American elders made the space sacred, and Louis Farrakhan's young followers, dressed in tuxedos, guarded the ballroom where the major events happened. A pair of young men stood at every door. "You will be safe," they promised.

For almost a week we talked about population trends, interfaith dialogue, sharing the earth's resources, and moving in the direction of world peace, getting to know each other as genuine colleagues. I had a great time. In the major assemblies I was often the only woman seated among the Buddhist monks, a gray-robed monk in a sea of saffron robes. Only later did I realize how difficult it must have been for the Theravada monks who surrounded me. They're not supposed to touch women or be touched by them. And yet when I'm excited I'm like a puppy: everyone is my best friend and merits a hug. I can only imagine their relief when the week was over.

During the parliament I met hundreds of monks and escorted groups of them around downtown Chicago. I even ate lunch with Arlo Guthrie. We ended up sharing a booth in a diner because the wait was so long for tables. He ate while I stared, remembering every single word to "Alice's Restaurant," the song that had introduced him to the world. For the first time in my life I didn't eat the french fries in front of me. Both Arlo and the monks, to a person, were a delight—sparkly eyed, kind, grinning. One old tiger called me "Smiley Girl" every time he saw me, which was often. We were best friends for a week.

Almost ten years later I saw one of the Theravada monks again. Now one of the leaders of a national Buddhist organization, he attended a Hindu-Buddhist dialogue that I also attended—an extravaganza put on by one of Detroit's largest Hindu temples. Detroit is a city of faith. Within blocks of us are a Christian Science church, several Baptist churches, a huge Congregational church, and a historic Catholic church. Across the street, an Islamic temple. Fundamentalist Christians live beside Jews, beside Muslims, beside us.

I had been asked, before the Hindu-Buddhist dialogue, to give the keynote speech. The event organizer was a kind of "nonrobed monk," a devoted follower of Hinduism. He was sweet and eager about the dialogue, convinced that simply putting people of different religious traditions in a room together would benefit both.

The topic for the keynote was the life of Buddha. I had worked hard to prepare a formal presentation, but when I stood at the podium and looked out at the sea of people—over a third of whom were children—I realized that my prepared remarks would be inappropriate. In that instant I came up with a totally different presentation, asking the children to whistle whenever I moved from one idea to the next (to make sure that I *did* move), and at one point pretending that we were all ten and a half months pregnant, like Buddha's mother just before giving birth.

> "A woman cannot be considered
> well versed in the Dharma
> just because she talks about it."

The presentation went over pretty well, at least for me and the kids. As soon as I was done, though, I started the self-criticism: "I should have been more formal." "The presentation was an introduction to Buddhism for many of the people there. What will they think now, after that foolishness?" "I forgot to thank the organizers—a mortal sin for presenters." Because I was conducting the postmortem late at night, I was tired enough to keep going: "I should have done a better job with ritual. My chanting was too fast."

Just as I hit my stride in the land of self-criticism, I noticed the Theravada monk standing behind me. He suddenly hit the back of my chair hard. Once. Twice. Three times. In an instant I was back to "just this" practice, back to *now*. The criticisms disappeared like fast-moving clouds.

He looked right into my eyes and smiled. Suddenly it was dharma Olympics, and I'd just performed my first swan dive.

"Ten points," he said.

"Ten points."

THE PATH
The spiritual path
is the Eightfold Path.
The truths
are the Four Noble Truths.

This is the path
for purity of vision.
Following it protects you
from temptation.

Following this path
leads to the end
of suffering.
This truth was
declared
once Buddha learned
how to pull the arrow out
of suffering.

You must do your own work.
A Buddha can only guide you.

By entering the path
seekers can transcend
all pain.

When, through your own effort,
you see that
everything
arises and passes away,
you will see the true nature
of suffering
and be able to let go of it.
This is the path to purity.

When, through your own effort,
you see that
all dharmas are impersonal,
you will be able to let go
of attachment.
This is the path to purity.

The person who does not do the work
when she is young and strong—
the person who is idle,
loose in how he spends
his days
and in what he thinks—
that lazy one will never find
the path to freedom.

Be heedful of your words,
restrained in your thinking.

Do not let your body harm.
Do these things sincerely
and you will attain freedom
just as the Buddha did.

Wisdom grows out of effort.
Without effort wisdom wanes.
Knowing this,
spend your days
in a way
that will allow wisdom
to surface.

Cut down the forest
of passions,
not just the trees.
Attachment grows out of passions
and fear.
Cutting down both trees and brush
frees you from both.

If the roots
of your attachments
are not completely pulled out,
even the smallest remainder
will keep you in bondage
like a suckling calf
that cannot live without its mother.
As if they were autumn lilies,
cut off your attachments
even to yourself.

Cultivate the path of peace,
the path of Nirvana,
the path taught by Buddha.

"Here's where I'll live now."
"There's where I'll live later."
In this way fools make plans,
not giving a thought
to their own dying.

Death cuts each of us off
while we are busy being
distracted by our lives.
Caring only for our livelihoods
and our children,
we are like sleeping towns
that end up being swept away
by flash floods.

Nobody can save us from our own dying:
not our parents,
not our children,
not even our best friend.
No one.

Knowing this,
be virtuous
and wise.
Surrender
to the spiritual practice
that leads to your awakening.

Happy Birthday, Buddhas

I asked one of the dharma students, playwright and poet Ron Allen, if he would tell the story of Buddha's birth for our Buddha's birthday celebration.

He wrote the following skit:

BUDDHA'S BIRTHDAY

KOHO: the human race is doomed bad attitudes bad ineffective deodorant tooth decay miserable weather pill-popping depressions bad feet alienation subjugation and unsightly hair needing repair.

KOGAM: the human race is in trouble/seeing double/multiple root facial warts, people's court and bad personalities and of course, ego trauma, ego karma, ego inflation in the nation

KAREN: we need a weapon

KEVIN: we need a weapon

P'ARANG: we need a god we need a theory not a weapon, we need to lighten up, we need the sixfold path

ALL: we need a drum, we need to lighten up

RON: then there was music *(group plays instruments)*

DREW: we need the empty

ALL: we need a gong, we need an event

KEVIN: the sixfold path just doesn't sound right

CAT: how about the shining path

DREW: we need the empty

P'ARANG: maybe the word *fold* isn't right, the seven-course path

ALL: we need a drum

KAREN: I know what we need, the three noble path or better the four mediocre lies

ALICE: we need the four global clues

ALL: we need a weapon

DREW: we need the empty

SARA: I really think it's the eight-track path

KOHO: the human race is doomed

KOGAM: it's all over we are doomed to ignorance

P'ARANG: I got it we need the greatfold path

SARA: I think you dudes are crazy we need the four-four blues

RON and CAT: there is an unidentified object fast approaching earth

KAREN: can you see what it is

CAT: I can't tell it looks like it's following an eightfold path

ALL *(playing instruments):* all hail the unidentified object

DREW: it's the empty . . . , coming

KEVIN: I can see it has a large stomach

KAREN: and it's smiling

KOGAM: it's the one noble truth

ALICE: it's still unidentified but it might be the weapon

RON: traveling at a rate of nothing for twenty-five hundred years

ALL *(playing instruments):* all hail the nothing

SARA: I can see it, it looks like P'arang, no it's not P'arang, it's P'arang with a haircut

JOE: it's the four hopeful gurus

ALICE: I can't see it but it must be the one

JOE: we need to lighten up

Koho: it's the light

All *(playing instruments):* it's the light

Drew: no . . . empty is here

Ron: the unidentified object is about to be identified we are about to lighten up

Joe: it looks like a Buddha

Alice: it looks like us

Sara: it's the path . . . eightfold

Kogam: we are going to lighten up with Buddha

Drew: listen it's the empty

P'arang: I remember now the eightfold path

Koho: that object looks a lot like Kogam

Karen: the Four Noble Truths

All: yes the Eightfold Path the Four Noble Truths

Joe: that object looks suspiciously like Sara

Karen: It's Kevin

Joe: I'm Buddha

Alice: I'm Buddha

Koho: I'm Buddha

Sara: I'm Buddha

P'arang: I'm Buddha

Koho: I'm Buddha

Kogam: I'm Buddha

Cat: I'm Buddha

Ron: I'm Buddha

All: I'm Buddha

Ron: the unidentified object has been recognized as Buddha coming to celebrate our birthday, so lighten up and celebrate

Drew: the next page to the play is empty I knew I was right

All *(playing instruments, shouting):* happy birthday, Buddhas

MISCELLANEOUS
By giving up a lesser happiness
one may gain a much greater one.
Let the wise give up the lesser
to attain the greater.

A person who seeks
her own happiness
by inflicting pain on others
ends up caught in hatred.

By doing things
that should not be done
and not doing things
that should be done,
the arrogant and unmindful
will only deepen their corruptions.

Those who earnestly practice
mindfulness will be aware
of what they are doing.
They will not do things
that should not be done.

Instead they will do
what needs doing.
As a result
their corruptions will dissipate.

Having killed craving
and conceit,
having let go
of attachment,
the holy ones have no
regrets.

Having killed craving
and conceit,
having destroyed the hindrances to
their practice,
the holy ones have
no regrets.

From the time they arise,
throughout the day,
until they go to sleep,
the followers of Buddha
constantly
take refuge in him.

From the time they arise,
throughout the day,
until they go to sleep,
the followers of Buddha
constantly
take refuge in the Dharma.

From the time they arise,
throughout the day,
until they go to sleep,
the followers of Buddha
constantly
take refuge in the Sangha.

From the time they arise,
throughout the day,
until they go to sleep,
the followers of Buddha
know not to be attached
to their bodies.

From the time they arise,
throughout the day,
until they go to sleep,
the followers of Buddha
delight in doing no harm.

From the time they arise,
throughout the day,
until they go to sleep,
the followers of Buddha
delight in meditation.

It is hard
to be wholly spiritual.
It is difficult
to delight in practicing spirituality
all the time.
But our earthly lives are also hard,

and associating with people
who are not spiritual
can be difficult as well.

The main point is this:
woe befalls people who live
a completely worldly life.
Do not pursue
a life of woe.

A person who is confident
and virtuous,
who has fame and wealth,
is honored
wherever he may go.

Like the Himalayas
the good are visible
even from afar.
Like bullets shot in the night
the wicked cannot be seen
even if they are
right next to us.

Those who—
with great energy—
sit alone,
rest alone,
walk alone,
and control themselves
will find delight in the forest.

Mudslinging in Dharmaland

"From the time they arise,
throughout the day,
until they go to sleep,
the followers of Buddha
delight in doing no harm."

Just before I was ordained as a dharma teacher in 1995, I read somewhere that spiritual leaders always have to deal with people coming at them. They have to face attacks on credibility, on morals, on ethics. Pretty much anywhere there's an opening, someone will appear to berate, belittle, shout, denounce. It was scary to read a prediction that no matter what I did, people would attack. I'm a lover, not a fighter.

It used to drive my mother nuts. All through grade school I got into trouble. I was little and mouthy, so someone was invariably beating me up for something. Usually my antagonist was Donny Beverly. I fought back only once, and that was solely because my mother shouted at my two little sisters to "get out there and stick up for your sister." I was six years old at the time.

Since then I've continued to hate fighting—*any* fighting. I can count the number of real arguments I've had on both hands. My mantra? There's always a peaceful way out of a tough situation.

For those of us who founded Still Point, that belief was paramount. In part to position ourselves to always take the peaceful tack, we started the temple with a strong code of ethics:

THE STILL POINT ZEN BUDDHIST TEMPLE CODE OF ETHICS

Because the foundation of spiritual life depends on mindful and caring relationship to the life around us, the following precepts constitute this temple's code of ethics:

1. We undertake the precept of nonviolence. We agree that violence of any kind undermines the core teaching of Buddhism: that all beings are precious.

2. We undertake the precept of refraining from stealing. We agree to bring consciousness to the use of all of the earth's resources in a respectful and ecological way. We agree to be honest in our dealing with money and not to misappropriate money committed to dharma projects.

3. We undertake the precept of refraining from sexual misconduct. We agree to avoid creating harm through sexuality and to avoid sexual exploitation or adultery. A sexual relationship is never appropriate between teachers and students when they are in a teacher/student relationship.

4. We undertake the precept of refraining from false speech. We agree to make every effort to speak that which is true and useful and refrain from gossip. We agree to hold in confidence what is explicitly told to us in confidence. We agree to cultivate conscious and clear communication, and to cultivate the qualities of lovingkindness and honesty as the basis of our speech.

5. We undertake the precept of refraining from the use of intoxicants. It is clear that substance abuse is a cause of tremendous suffering. We agree that there should be no use of intoxicants while on temple or retreat premises. We agree not to abuse or misuse intoxicants at any time. We agree that if any teacher has a drug or alcohol addiction problem, it should be immediately addressed by the community.

The code is publicly posted so that everyone in the community can hold me accountable for my behavior and so that we can all be accountable to each other. I figured that the code's explicit guidelines would serve as a shield of armor.

Wrong.

The attacks started early. First, several spiritual leaders from different traditions showed up, a few at a time, over the course of a few weeks, for services. They stood at the back of the meditation hall, watching everything we did and frowning their disapproval. I invited them back, but they never came.

Then Daniel, a well-known neighborhood resident, started criticizing us to anyone who would listen. Usually he'd be sitting on the ledge of our host-church's porch when he did it. Sometimes just seeing the first few people walk up the porch stairs to come to a Sunday service was enough to get him started. "All these people," he'd say to me. "All these people come from the suburbs in their nice cars. You think they help Detroit. They *don't* help Detroit! I ask them for money. Ask them for food. Nobody gives me money. Well, just once—and I really needed it too. Your people just come here for mental masturbation!"

By now this is an old rant, but it's still aired regularly. I've heard it at least a half-dozen times, sometimes as I'm making him lunch at the abbey.

A couple of Sundays ago, Daniel was at his best when I noticed him at his usual post, chatting with someone, and went out to talk with him before the service. We tend to have fairly friendly conversations because he actually likes us when he's not mad at me for telling him he could work, that the neighborhood has jobs he could do. (He could help us paint the abbey, for example, and we'd pay him.) That day he would have none of it.

"Yup, all you people do is mental masturbation."

On the other side of me, leaning against the brick wall, is a young man, maybe in his twenties. His long blond hair is as filthy as the rest of him. I could write my name with a fingernail on his arm, it's so caked with dirt. His face is streaked with sweat stains. He's just finished telling me that he took a bus from Saginaw to visit his ailing grandmother in Detroit. It's unclear how he'll get back home. At the phrase "mental masturbation," he perks up.

"Zen mental masturbation?"

Daniel starts in again.

"Yup. People from the suburbs come here for it and then go back to their safe suburbs."

Suddenly Ango is standing beside me.

"I don't," he says.

"I don't," I say.

"Yeah," says Daniel. Ango and I go inside to meditate, and when we come out again the two are gone.

Attacks. The next one came when a monk from a different sangha announced that I "feed people's egos instead of breaking them." Okay. I could handle that. We certainly do have different styles. Using the strings of a lute as a metaphor, Buddha used to say that teachings should be neither too taut nor too loose. The other monk is taut relative to me. I'm loose relative to him. His was useful feedback.

The next round came from a disgruntled sangha member. "She's too unsure" was the judgment against me. "She's not a real Zen master." I could live with those opinions as well. I promised myself that I would keep checking in for sincerity and do extra practice to stay upright and focused.

But then my former teacher got into the game. For the most part that monk had been a wonderful teacher for me. His dharma talks rocked. The retreats he led were powerful; they sliced through ego. I had only one problem with him: he put on the best tantrums of anyone I'd ever seen. True theater. After more than twelve years as his student, though, I finally left, unconvinced that, in the end, the tantrums were anything but abuse. (I've had enough experience to know.)

After I left, I got a stream of reports of denouncements and harangues uttered by this teacher in my name. I didn't get overly concerned over any of them, assuming that this was just the monk being the monk. Then came a frontal attack, a printed "clarification" of my qualifications in his newsletter. While I'm ordained, he said, I'm not "a full-fledged teacher." That was the first time I'd heard that expression in the years I'd known the man. Then he linked me to a suicide of one of our dearest sangha members.

Rumors of the clarification started circulating the day this monk's newsletter first became available to the public. My immediate reaction was fury. How dare he?! I wanted to sue, to take the man to court, to make internet banners denouncing him back. What a jerk! I had the higher moral ground, and I knew it. Forget peaceful solutions! I wanted a public fistfight. A bully is a bully, even when he's dressed in monks' robes.

> "By giving up a lesser happiness
> one may gain a much greater one.

Let the wise give up the lesser
to attain the greater."

I was obsessed. Revenge fantasies kept cropping up in my practice, even as I fought them back. So I just did more practice, trading meditation in for reciting the three refuges:

- I go for refuge to the Buddha and resolve that with all beings I will realize the Great Way and develop a heart of enlightenment.

- I go for refuge to the Dharma and resolve that with all beings I will penetrate the teachings and uncover wisdom as vast as the ocean.

- I go for refuge to the Sangha and resolve that with all beings I will seek great peace and harmony so that nothing will impede our progress toward an enlightened society.

Over and over and over. I chanted until I could sit down to write a letter without frothing at the mouth. "What you did was wrong," I penned. "The Dharma deserves better." And then, thanks to years of practice, I really could let go, realizing that the monk was still acting as a great teacher to me. Someone will always be frustrated with me, angry about something I've done. I make mistakes. We *all* do. The only thing any of us can offer back is a sincere heart, growing wisdom, and all the energy we can muster. Still Point gets all three. Buddha will take care of the rest.

REALMS OF WOE
Those who are in the habit
of telling lies
and those who do things
that they then claim they didn't do
are equal after death.
Both end up in hell.

Some spiritual leaders have
evil dispositions.
They are unrestrained in
thought, word, and deed.
Because of these evil things
they are reborn
in hell.

It is better to swallow
a red-hot iron ball
that burns like a flame
than to eat food
respectfully offered by others
if one is immoral

and unrestrained
in thought, word, and deed.

Four kinds of misfortune come to those
who commit adultery:
bad karma,
disturbed sleep,
and a bad reputation
are already known.
To these add the risk
of being reborn in hell.

Trading bad karma
and bad destiny
for the brief joy of adultery
brings heavy punishment.
Do not consort with
someone else's partner.

In the same way that
a piece of glass
grasped carelessly
cuts your hand,
carelessness about moral behavior
leads to hell.

Loose acts,
corrupt practices,
questionable holiness:
none of these
brings good fruit.

If you are going to do something,
give yourself completely to
whatever it is
and stick with it
steadily.
Halfhearted efforts
just make more mess.

It is better not to do an evil deed
in the first place—
it will only torment you later.
Better to do a good deed
you will not regret.

Like a city on a country's border
guarded both inside and out,
guard yourself.
Do not waste this life.
Those who let their lives
slip away
grieve
when they are reborn in hell.

Those ashamed of purity
have it all wrong.
Those who fear the harmless
but see no harm in danger
have it all wrong.
Embracing wrong views,
they are reborn in hell.

Those who imagine evil
where there is none
but do not see evil
where it exists
have it all wrong.
Embracing wrong views,
they are reborn in hell.

Those who know
wrong is wrong
and right is right—
embracing right views
they fall into bliss.

Four Kinds of Misfortune

"Loose acts,
corrupt practices,
questionable holiness:
none of these
brings good fruit."

In the course of a short period, several women called Still Point asking to meet with me. Although none of them was connected to the temple, each was referred by a sangha member. To a person, they had the same story to tell: their mates were having affairs.

In one instance the infidelity came after more than twenty years of a great marriage, a partnership of equals. A young colleague had gone to the woman's husband for advice. The next thing the caller knew, her husband and the young colleague were "soul mates" spending hours together each day. "What should I do?" she asked me.

The second woman had been married for only two years. This was her second marriage, his first. A lifelong bachelor, he was having trouble settling down. For the past two months he'd been making an unusually large number of business trips to Toronto. She was convinced that he was seeing someone.

"How do you know?" I asked.

"I read his emails."

The third woman's story was so close to the first woman's that meeting with her felt a little like watching the movie *Groundhog Day*. She and her partner, another woman, had been together for years. They'd been best friends as well as lovers. For almost a year, though, her partner had been eating lunch more and more often with a woman at work. Some weeks it was every day. Just the two of them. Recently the partner had started phoning home several nights a week to say that she'd be working late. As this third woman sat in Still Point's office and talked of her pain, she said that she just *knew* her partner was having an affair.

"Why?" I asked.

"It's the way her eyes light up when she talks about her new friend," she said.

My heart breaks for all of them. Adultery is the worst betrayal. It destroys so much in its wake—not just that one relationship, but friendships, relationships with other family members, with children. Buddha singled out adultery as a special obstacle to spiritual growth. In his lifetime, his good friend King Pasenadi fell so in love with a young woman that he plotted the death of her husband so that he could have her all to himself. Fortunately (although I think I can safely say that *he* didn't see good fortune in the turn of events), the king was haunted by ear-shattering moaning and groaning in the castle as he schemed. The sounds so terrified him that he went to Buddha for advice. What should he do?

Buddha told him that the ghosts were men who had committed adultery in their lifetimes. The hell they had landed in was so gruesome that the sound of their pain crossed from hell into the human realm. The combination of the sounds and Buddha's reply was enough for the king to give up his fantasy before carrying out the murder. He concluded that if the consequences in this lifetime weren't painful enough, landing in one of the worst hells was sufficient incentive to think twice about his scheme.

"Four kinds of misfortune come to those
who commit adultery:
bad karma,
disturbed sleep,
and a bad reputation
are already known.
To these add the risk
of being reborn in hell."

The adulterous behavior of the partners described earlier was deeply harmful. On the other hand, I've never known a person who just woke up one morning and said to himself or herself, "Today I'll fall in love with someone and start an affair." Such relationships grow from small seeds of attraction that take root and grow as they are watered, interaction by interaction. Knowing this can be strong preventive medicine, reminding us that interactions within a field of attraction need to be kept impersonal.

To tell you the truth, I didn't really know what to say to the women who came to me with their concerns about fidelity. Every cell in my body wanted to judge the adulterers who'd hurt them. Boiling oil felt about right. *How dare they?!* I thought indignantly. *How dare they hurt someone who loves them so?* Just as my mind started to settle on channel RIGHTEOUSNESS, I stopped. Who among us hasn't betrayed someone who loves us? Be honest now. Maybe we've just *noticed* other people, or maybe we've flirted in line at the grocery store. Maybe we've told the secrets of our relationship to someone else, breaking our vow of intimacy the way a rock thrown into a pond disturbs the water's clear quiet. Buddha's words haunted me as I thought about the women's predicaments. Hate never dispels hate, he said. Only love dispels hate. With each woman that message was the tape that played in my mind at the moment when I wanted to let loose with a string of furious words.

Heartbreak hurt like hell. I let the women know that I understood that. Then I suggested that they be sure about their fears—that they were based on fact, not fiction. If the adultery was confirmed, the women then needed to renegotiate their relationship if they could. To lay clear ground rules. To forgive if they could and move on if they couldn't. To move on for sure if no end of the affair was in sight. Mostly, though, I urged them to be kind to themselves and as kind as they could be to their mates.

And then?

Then I just cried with them. For all of us.

THE ELEPHANT
Just as an elephant in a battlefield
endures the arrows shot from a bow,
I too will endure abuse.
Indeed, many people in this world
harm.

Only the best-trained elephants
are taken into battlefields.
In the same way,
only those who best train themselves
spiritually
can withstand abuse.

Better than trained mules,
thoroughbred horses,
or noble, tusked elephants
are those who have trained themselves.

There is no mode of transportation
that can take a person
to Nirvana.

Only by controlling one's senses
and training one's mind
can that goal be reached.

During the mating season
the mighty elephant Dhanapalaka
will not eat a morsel of food
and is uncontrollable.
Held in captivity
he can only
dream of home
among
the other elephants.

A foolish person,
someone who is lazy,
gluttonous,
and sleepy—
who wallows in his or her life
like a huge hog
nourished on slop—
is doomed
to repeated rebirths.

My mind used to wander
wherever it wanted,
whenever it wanted.
Now, through mindfulness,
I control it, keep it
in check—
as an elephant who,

even in the mating season,
is controlled by a trainer.

Delight in mindfulness.
Guard your mind well.
In the same way that
an elephant stuck in mud
pulls itself out, pull yourself
out of the mud
of moral defilements.

If you can find a virtuous companion
to live with you,
a companion who is
well behaved and wise,
live with him
joyfully and mindfully.

But if you cannot find a virtuous
companion fit to live with you—
if you can't find someone
who behaves well and is wise—
then, like a king
who leaves his kingdom,
live alone
like an elephant in a forest.

It is better to live
alone
than to have fellowship with fools.
Let yourself live

alone,
doing no evil,
carefree,
like an elephant in the forest.

It is good
to have friends
when one is in need.
It is good
to be content
with whatever is.
It is good
to have merit
when life is about to end.
It is good
to let go of sorrow.

In this world
it is good
to be dutiful
to one's mother,
dutiful
to one's father,
helpful
to people on a spiritual path,
and helpful
to the enlightened ones.

It is good to stay virtuous
into old age.
It is good to have unshakable faith.
It is good to gain wisdom.
It is good to be free.

Jack the Duck and the Bodhisattva of Compassion

"Better than trained mules,
thoroughbred horses,
or noble, tusked elephants
are those who have trained themselves."

The abbey is becoming a petting farm. First, two chickens. Ango rescued them from the Eastern Market so that they wouldn't be someone's Sunday dinner. We even have a picture of one of them, Tragedy, posted on our bulletin board. Then some mice. Too many mice, actually. In fact, we all agreed that our compassionate mouse-catching technique (which involves putting candies in the bottom of a paper bag, waiting for a mouse to leap in, covering said bag and mouse with a cookie sheet, and hauling the trespasser out to a vacant lot) wasn't keeping up with all the mouse sex going on, so we decided to get a temple cat. That's when Neptune, who needed a home anyway, joined our family.

But the petting farm didn't stop there. For Easter, Cat's sister gave her a baby duckling. She named it Jack Keroquack. Cat cautiously made his presence known, unsure of our reactions. Since we didn't have an abbey protocol regarding ducks, she wasn't sure what any of us would do. Jack was an adorable ball of furlike feathers, and we all fell in love with him immediately. Even so, she promised that he would be at the abbey for only about a month or so.

That was a while ago. He never stopped being cute (though he *did* have a negative impact on our basement, as I mentioned in an earlier chapter). We watched him learn how to get in and out of the plastic toddler pool that Cat put out for him—not as easy a task as you might expect. He'd struggle to climb in, only to attack all of the orange-colored sections of the pool. Enemy beaks. Then, getting out, he'd fall on his face and straighten up clumsily, looking dazed. This went on for weeks. We laughed ourselves silly watching him.

Outsiders took pleasure in his antics too. People who came to the abbey to talk about problems with their practice—which often turned into conversations about the problems in their lives—would soften as they watched him. One Thursday night a man came to the temple wound so tightly with rage and heartbreak that I knew he wouldn't be able to meditate, even though that was why he had appeared at the door. I asked him if he'd mind sitting on the back porch for a couple of minutes while I got the meditation room ready for him. When I went to tell him it was ready, he was watching Jack. Although he was laughing, a tiny stream of tears rolled down each cheek. I left man and duck alone for a while longer, figuring that Jack had more healing capacity than I'd realized.

Jack thought Cat was his mother. He followed her around faithfully. When spring showed up in earnest, Cat decided to start leaving Jack in the back yard for the day, so that he'd have room to roam. As she walked around with him that first day, he wouldn't leave her side, and he was reluctant to see her go. Later that day, alone, he discovered the statue of Quan Yin (the bodhisattva of compassion).

The owners of Falling Water Books and Collectables, a sweet healing store in Ann Arbor, had given us a three-foot, pale gray statue of the Buddhist saint just before we got Jack. She looks a lot like Mary, the mother of Jesus, in her robes with her small smile. When we got her I wasn't sure where to put her, so I stuck her on a patch of grass about four feet out from our back porch, figuring that the abbot or one of the sangha's master gardeners would move her to her rightful place. Within the week, however, two people at a Saturday retreat put her on a small pedestal and surrounded her with plants. Suddenly we had a Quan Yin shrine.

By the end of his first day alone Jack decided that Quan Yin was his real mother. Cat had been just a surrogate. To this day, he sits right next to the statue for big chunks of the day. Apparently she's teaching him everything he needs to know. During his first hard rain, he ran to her side from across the yard and she gave him shelter. When a new visitor came rushing down the back stairs to pet him, he ducked behind Quan Yin. He knew she wouldn't budge. She didn't. When a police siren started blaring just outside the gate, he ran to Quan Yin, resting his head on her pedestal, safe from the sound. Again, she was fearless. Gradually, taking cues from her, Jack is growing his own courage. More and more, when there's a new person or sound, he stops, watches, and sits like a mountain, just like his mother.

> "If you can find a virtuous companion
> to live with you,
> a companion who is
> well behaved and wise,
> live with him
> joyfully and mindfully."

C H A P T E R

24

CRAVING
The craving of a person
addicted to careless living grows
like a runaway vine.
Such a person jumps
from life to life
like a monkey jumping
from tree to tree,
looking for fruit.

If you are overcome by craving,
your sorrows will grow
like weeds
after a hard rain.

Whoever overcomes this
wretched craving
will experience her sorrows
falling away from her
like water dropping
from a leaf
or a flower.

So I say to you: Greetings
to all who have assembled here!
Dig up your roots
of craving,
just as someone who wants
beautiful flowers
digs up weeds.
Do not let temptation
destroy you
again and again
as a flood overwhelms a reed.

In the same way that
a felled tree
sprouts
again if its roots stay
strong,
suffering will arise
again and again
if the roots of craving
are not completely destroyed.

A person who gives way to pleasure
will be swept away by craving.
His thoughts will become
an ocean of suffering.

The streams of craving
flow everywhere,
sending out strands
like a creeper vine.

Seeing your own craving,
cut it off at its roots
with wisdom.

A person's joys
are always transient,
and since we tend
to devote ourselves
to pleasure,
our seeking after happiness
leads us to
repeated birth and decay.

People controlled by craving
become terrified,
rabbits caught in snares.
A person
who wants peace
needs to eradicate craving.

Having let go of the forest
of desire, a person
can take up a forest
of practice.
Without mindfulness, though,
even after freeing ourselves
from craving,
we can find ourselves
rushing back
into that very thicket.

Prisons made of
iron, wood, or stone
pale
in comparison to the longing for
jewels,
ornaments,
mates,
and children.
Attachments are far stronger prisons,
say the wise.

The bond of attachment
ties you
completely,
even though the knots may
feel loose.
The wise let go of their
longings
before they die.

People who are infatuated
with lust
fall back into the stream
of suffering,
just like a spider falling
into its own web.
The wise, cutting off
the bonds of craving,
walk on resolutely,
leaving all
sorrow behind.

Let go of the past!
Let go of the future!
Let go of now!
Crossing beyond the shore
of existences,
with a mind freed of all
conditioned thinking,
you will no longer
face another birth or death.

Craving builds in one who
becomes lustful on seeing beauty.
In such a person
the bond of desire
grows stronger.

On the other hand,
the person who
understands that the body is
merely a collection of organs,
and who is constantly mindful—
that person will end craving.
She will sever desire's bond.

The man
who has freed himself
from craving
is fearless.
He has cut off the thorns of life.
This is his final body.

The woman who is
free from craving,
from attachment,
who is skilled in language
and understands the significance
of letting go of desire,
is indeed
one who has lived her last life—
a woman of great wisdom,
a great woman.

Having uprooted craving,
I have overcome every desire.
I understand.
I am detached.
I have let go.
I have freed myself from
moral defilements.
Truly understanding
the Four Noble Truths,
who shall I call teacher?

Truth
is the best of all gifts.
The flavor of truth
is beyond sweet.
The pleasure of truth
is the best of all pleasures.
The person who
has destroyed desire
has overcome all sorrow.

Wanting wealth destroys the foolish,
but not those who seek
Nirvana.
By craving riches
the fool destroys
himself
in the same way
that he would destroy
his enemies.

Weeds can destroy fields.
Desire spoils lives.
Honor those
who have freed themselves
from desire.

Weeds can destroy fields.
Hatred spoils all beings.
Be generous to those
who have freed themselves
from hatred.

Weeds can destroy fields.
Delusion spoils all beings.
Honor those
who have freed themselves
from delusion.

Weeds can destroy fields.
Craving destroys all beings.
Be generous to those

who have freed themselves
from craving.
Your generosity
will be repaid
over
and over.

The Middle Way

In the early 1990s one of my best friends had a knack for falling in love with either difficult or unavailable women. One time he asked our teacher what he could do about his obsession with a particular red-haired woman who had started coming to the temple. I don't think he was the only one distracted by her. She augmented her natural beauty with form-fitting spandex pants and shorts. I felt sorry for the men and women who had to follow her in walking meditation. Concentration would be hard.

> "If you are overcome by craving,
> your sorrows will grow
> like weeds
> after a hard rain."

Our teacher's solution to my friend's problem was immediate: "One thousand prostrations!"

My friend didn't respond quite so quickly, but within days he'd done his thousand prostrations—full-bodied bows to the floor. On a good day that many can be done in about three hours. It's like running a marathon up steep hills. At their finish, he was still obsessed, however. Disappointed, he headed back to our teacher.

"One thousand more!"

This time, either the prostrations helped or my friend decided to keep his problem to himself. (He later told me that the remedy had helped. I believe him.)

We grasp and we crave. That's our human nature. And yet if we stick to our meditation practice, it uproots the grasping and craving that call our mind home. Meditation has a way of shining a light on things so that we can see ourselves clearly.

Every spring, as Still Point sangha members prepare for our precept-taking ceremony, we discuss a different precept each Sunday. Each time at least some of the discussion heads in the direction of talking about the patterns of craving we're noticing.

While sex is at the top of many lists, craving cuts a wide swath. Some of us crave certain foods. I, for one, can't imagine a life without chocolate at least once a week. Someone else talks about the internet. Mexican food. Pizza. Some of us crave neatness or having other people in our families live by our ground rules. One or two of us still crave shopping sprees or alcohol. We *all* crave living. It's amazing how prominent a part craving plays in our everyday life.

After each of these conversations in the spring, I tend to get a couple of phone calls within the next week: "I'm going to go to Alcoholics Anonymous. Just wanted you to know." Or, "I've made a promise to cut back to one cup of coffee a day." Or, "I've cut up all my credit cards except my VISA."

I'm thrilled for the callers. They're on their way to a sane life.

Outside of an insatiable lust for breathing, my last great addiction is for chocolate. It's downright scary when there isn't any in the abbey. Over time I've learned to watch the craving take form. It usually starts as a feeling of being thirsty, though my tongue says, "Close, but not quite," when I get myself a drink of water. When liquid isn't satisfying, my brain immediately kicks in, suggesting, "Chocolate would be good."

Mostly, just sitting with the craving makes it go away—a storm front CLEAR followed by I WANT CHOCOLATE followed by CLEAR. No need to fight it, no need to act, just sit. Every once in a while, though, sitting doesn't do it. Usually it's when I'm tired from an intense week. Perhaps I've chanted someone through her dying or spent time with someone in the hospital. Perhaps one of the sangha members just can't let go of something and has had to talk about it with me every day. When my goodwill is pretty much gone and my system is in overdrive, I often go find a handful of M&Ms or a chocolate bar to eat.

This is the middle way, after all. Buddha taught that extreme asceticism can be just as damaging as living a life of indulgence. As in the story of Goldilocks and the three bears, in which one porridge was just right, our lives also have a middle ground. While too much chocolate is harmful, no chocolate at all can be just as problematic. I might, for example, be obsessed about chocolate, or I might feed my ego with self-satisfaction from having the willpower to just say no. Both extremes are attachments. I'm convinced that in every situation there's a middle way, and that the "just right" point is different for all of us (and in fact is different at different times for all of us). That's part of what makes this path so juicy!

Take alcohol. One person's middle way might be a single drink or a couple of beers. Given that I'm a slobbery, giggly drunk after one glass of wine, my middle way is *no* alcohol. My system just can't handle it. Situations shift the point, however: sometimes a handful of chocolates keeps me upright, but sometimes—say, when I'm especially tired—that same handful makes me edgy, even anxious.

Other times I just know, at the core of me, that chocolate isn't a good idea. I've been eating too much lately, perhaps, or I've already had lots of sugar that day. If simply sitting with the craving doesn't help, it's to the nearest altar I go. Time for prostrations.

Within twenty minutes the craving is generally gone. And some of my energy is back—enough to trade in chocolate for a big glass of water. Enough to keep my chocolate stash whole for the next rough week.

> "Whoever overcomes this
> wretched craving
> will experience her sorrows
> falling away from her
> like water dropping
> from a leaf
> or a flower."

25

THE MONK
Restrain your eyes.
Restrain your ears.
Restrain your nose.
Restrain your tongue.

Restrain your body.
Restrain your speech.
Restrain your mind.
In all instances, restraint is good.
The monk who is restrained
in every way
is freed from all suffering.

A person whose physical actions
are controlled,
who controls
where she goes
and what she says,
who delights in meditation,
is composed,
solitary,

and contented—
that woman they call blessed.

The monk who controls his tongue,
who speaks wisely,
mindfully,
who explains both
words and meaning—
sweet is his speech.

The monk who dwells in the Dharma,
delights in the Dharma,
meditates on the Dharma,
and remembers the Dharma well
does not fall away from it.

Do not dislike
gifts given to you,
nor envy the gain of others.
A person who envies others
cannot concentrate
on her spiritual practice.

Even if she gets just a little
caught up in gains and losses,
rather than sustaining
a purity of livelihood,
this woman the gods cannot praise.

A person who has no thoughts of
"I" and "mine"—

who is content—
deserves to be called *holy*.

The monk who personifies lovingkindness,
who is pleased with the teaching of Buddha,
attains a state of peace and happiness
where all conditioning is stilled.

Empty yourself!
This is the way to move swiftly
along a spiritual path.
Cutting off desire and ill will,
to Nirvana will you travel.

Cut off all fetters:
belief in a permanent personality;
skeptical doubt;
attachment to rules and rituals;
sensual craving;
ill will;
craving for birth in particular heavens;
conceit;
restlessness;
and psychological ignorance.

Cultivate the five faculties of faith:
enterprise;
mindfulness;
concentration;
insight;
and wisdom.

The monk who moves past
the things that bind him
is called "one who has crossed over."

Meditate!
Be heedful!
Do not let your mind get caught
in sensual pleasures.
Do not be so careless
that you unthinkingly swallow
something so harmful to you
that you can only cry out in pain.

Concentration is impossible
for a person who lacks wisdom.
Wisdom is impossible
for a person who lacks concentration.
When a person can concentrate
and is wise,
he is in the presence of
Nirvana.

The monk who has
retreated to an isolated spot,
who has calmed her mind,
and who clearly understands Buddha's teaching
experiences a joy that
transcends worldly happiness.

Whenever she can simply reflect
on the rise and fall of all things,

she experiences joy and happiness.
To "those who know," such reflection
is the deathless state.

The place to begin for a person
determined to be wise?
Control.
Contentment.
Restraint.
Association with beneficial and energetic friends.

Be with good friends.
Be amiable and correct in your own conduct.
Then, feeling great joy,
you will end the cycle of
rebirth.

Just as jasmine
sheds its withered petals,
so should you cast off
desire and ill will.

The monk who is
calm in body,
calm in speech,
and calm in mind,
who is well composed
and has given up worldly
things,
is truly peaceful.

Constantly monitor yourself.
Self-guarded and heedful,
you will live happily.

You are your own protector.
Indeed, you are your own refuge.
Therefore, control yourself
just as a skilled rider
controls a show horse.

Full of joy,
full of confidence in Buddha's teaching,
a person will attain the peaceful state—
where all conditioned elements
are stilled
and there is bliss.

The monk who, while still young,
devotes himself to Buddha's teaching
lights up the world
like the moon freed
from behind a cloud.

Lovingkindness

About ten years ago Mr. Kung called me up on a Saturday afternoon. No, "Hello, how are you?" just, "Come to lunch on Sunday with a monk." It was a rare request. He knew that I was crazy busy on Sundays. But Mr. Kung is Mr. Kung, so I went.

At the restaurant we were joined by a young Taiwanese monk, whom Mr. Kung introduced as Hui-min. As I greeted him I almost swooned. I was so immediately in love with him that I blushed. It was bizarre. He wasn't particularly handsome, I didn't know anything about him, and I don't think he'd even opened his mouth yet. And yet I was overwhelmed and confused by a rush of positive emotion.

> "The monk who personifies lovingkindness,
> who is pleased with the teaching of Buddha,
> attains a state of peace and happiness
> where all conditioning is stilled."

I had brought my partner along—a cowboy's cowboy, a "kill the bastards" construction entrepreneur. As we sat down to lunch, my cowboy decided to wax poetic about overpopulation and how people with IQs lower than a certain number should all be neutered. It went downhill from there. I was so stunned at his outburst that I just sat there, silenced for once.

Mr. Kung ignored my friend. His English wasn't so great anyway. Hui-min, on the other hand, listened carefully, not wanting to miss a word.

Finally, not being able to stand it anymore, I interrupted the monologue. "Hui-min! How do you deal with difficult people?"

He grinned from ear to ear.

"I learn from them."

He was loving every minute: he clearly liked my partner, clearly liked me, clearly liked *everyone*. He was my first genuine taste of lovingkindness.

For Hui-min, it was all okay.

We spent the rest of lunch talking about technology and about what it's like to be a monk in Taiwan. He showed us his Palm Pilot prototype and gave me a book about Vimalakirti, a great Buddhist saint. I had never met anyone so genuine as Hui-min. His positive energy was so strong that even the waitresses found excuses to hover around the table and the owner of the restaurant came over to sit with us briefly. My partner asked for the check.

Hui-min's life is busy but simple. He wakes up, practices, eats, works, sleeps. He's happy.

And yet for all these years he's been in my heart. After just one meeting.

Two weeks ago I flew to San Francisco for a book-signing. Actually, it was in Mountain View, a community south of the city that feels suspiciously like Tusita heaven for someone from the heart of Detroit. Clear, sunny, rich. I couldn't figure out if there were more BMWs or more Jaguars. Plenty of both, in any case. Most of the people on the street looked like young models for technology company ads.

I stayed in a bed-and-breakfast in Palo Alto. It was a wonderful, sprawling old house that smelled like my grandmother's home on the beach in Massachusetts.

At breakfast I met a half-dozen of the inn's other guests. We sat at a big round table, introducing ourselves one by one. The first woman was a marketing director for a pharmaceutical firm. Then came an international consultant, followed by a journalist. The woman next to me was a renowned nutritionist. She had given her two young sons money to start a dot-com business. They'd done so well that they'd purchased an apartment for her in New York City. A good one. She also modeled.

Then it was my turn.

"I'm a monk." Saying the words out loud to strangers—something I rarely do—I suddenly realized that I've finally become a monk for real. Not because I practice all the time but because I'm happy, really happy. I'm content. I trust Buddha, Dharma, and Sangha as refuges. I trust myself. With my whole heart I wish everyone I've ever known well. How did I get this lucky?

Though the breakfast group at the inn nodded politely at my introduction, they completely ignored me for the rest of the meal. I'm just not part of the dance they're dancing. I loved them for their unsureness, one or two of them for their arrogance. As I poured myself a cup of coffee, listening to their conversation, I realized that their reactions to me truly didn't matter. I got a total kick out of each person regardless of what they thought of me.

I loved the way the marketing director talked—her voice staccato and to the point; I enjoyed how the movement of her hands exactly matched the rhythm of her words, almost as if she were conducting herself. That the international consultant felt a need to stand up every time he talked was adorable. He wanted to make certain we paid attention to him. (We did.) The woman sitting beside me had a pale beauty that was ethereal. She was all pastels, even her eyes.

As each person got up to leave I smiled a genuine good-bye, unhurried and heartfelt. And each person smiled in return. California smiles. Wide.

Silently chanting my way into the morning, I thought of Huimin. He had it right.

> "Full of joy,
> full of confidence in Buddha's teaching,
> a person will attain the peaceful state—
> where all conditioned elements
> are stilled
> and there is bliss."

26

THE NOBLE ONE
Cut off the stream of craving
with diligence.
Abandon sense-desires.
Know the end of conditioned experience.
Know Nirvana.

With tranquility and insight-meditation
a noble one will move far
along the spiritual path,
and all the fetters that have been
holding him back
will pass away.

A person who is free of fear
and attachments,
who is unstressed
and free from moral defilements—
this person is a noble one.

The person who is meditative
and stainless,

who tackles her responsibilities
free from corruption;
the woman who has found stillness—
this person is a noble one.

The sun shines during the day.
The moon shines at night.
The king shines in his regalia.
The follower shines in meditation.
The Buddha, in his glory,
shines day and night.

Because she has rejected evil
she is called a noble one.
Because he lives in peace
he is called calm.
Because she gives up impurities
she is known as
someone who has uprooted
her defilements.

One should not physically harm a noble one,
nor should a noble one get angry
at someone who has struck him.
Shame on the person who hits!
Shame on the person who gives in to anger!

For someone who is noble,
not needing to retaliate
is a great gift.
When the mind

is weaned from desire,
when the intent to harm stops,
sorrow will subside.

The person who does no evil—
not with her body,
not with her speech,
not with her mind—
the person who is skilled
in all these ways:
her I call noble.

Anyone who helps you to understand
the teachings of Buddha
should be revered in the same way
that some traditions
revere sacrificial fire.

One does not become noble
by looking the part.
One does not become noble
by being born into the right family.
One does not become noble
just because she was lucky enough
to have a human birth.
But where both truth and wisdom exist
in a person,
that person is truly noble.

What's the use of shaving your head?
What's the point of dressing the part?

Inside you are overflowing
with desire,
and yet you dress like a
spiritual seeker.

A person who wears any type of clothing,
even rags,
who is lean,
whose effort is clear,
who can meditate alone
even in a forest:
him I call noble.

I do not call a person noble
just because he was born
into a wealthy family.
A person who continues to cling
to things,
people,
places,
and senses
I can only call dear.
Only a person freed of defilements,
a person who has cut off all clinging,
do I call noble.

He who has cut out all that holds him back,
who is fearless,
who has gone beyond all attachments:
him I call a noble one.

The person who has cut
the strap of hatred,
the rope of lust,
the cage of heresies,
who has thrown up
the crossbar of delusion,
who is enlightened:
him I call a noble one.

The person who deals with abuse
without anger,
whose patience is
undefeatable
by the strongest army:
her I call noble.

The person who is dutiful,
virtuous,
self-controlled,
free from anger,
and free from craving
will not need to live
as a human again:
him I call a noble one.

The person who does not cling
to sensuous pleasures:
her I call a noble one.

The person who,
in this world,
is able to end sorrow,

who puts down the burden of
his defilements
and is freed of them:
him I call a noble one.

She whose knowledge is deep,
who is wise,
who knows right from wrong
and acts accordingly,
who has awakened:
her I call a noble one.

Whoever detaches himself
both from the laity
and from spiritual wanderers
having simple needs:
him I call a noble one.

The person who has
completely given up
the use of force
with all beings,
weak or strong,
who neither harms
nor kills:
her I call a noble one.

The person who is friendly among the hostile,
peaceful among the violent,
unattached among the attached:
him I call a noble one.

The person in whom
desire, hatred, pride,
and detraction
have fallen away:
her I call a noble one.

He whose words are
gentle, instructive, and true,
the one who offends no one
through his speech:
him I call a noble one.

She who, in this world,
takes nothing that has not been
given to her—
long or short,
big or small,
good or bad:
her I call a noble one.

The person who has no desire
for this world
or the next,
who is free from craving
and moral defilements:
him I call a noble one.

He who has transcended
both good and bad,
and attachments as well,
who is free from sorrow,

stainless,
and pure:
him I call a noble one.

She who is as clear as the moon,
who is pure,
serene,
unperturbed,
who has destroyed craving
for becoming:
her I call a noble one.

He who has crossed
the dangerous swamp of passion,
the difficult road of defilements,
the ocean of life,
and the darkness of ignorance
has reached the other shore—
Nirvana.

She who practices tranquility,
heedfulness,
meditation,
who is free from craving
and doubt,
who clings to nothing
and remains in perfect peace:
her I call a noble one.

Giving up sense-desires,
he who has renounced the worldly life

and become a spiritual seeker;
he who has destroyed sense-desires
and has come to the end of
his existence:
him I call a noble one.

Giving up craving,
she who would renounce worldly life
and become a spiritual seeker;
she who has destroyed craving
and has come to the end of her existence:
her I call a noble one.

The Next Buddha?

Koho calls the abbey looking for Ango. "Hey, Koho!" I say. "Didn't you tell me you read somewhere that Maitreya, the next Buddha, won't be a person? That Maitreya will be sangha?"

"Thich Nhat Hanh says it in *Teachings on Love*," he says. "I have the quote right here." He reads to me: "We have to help the next Buddha, Maitreya, the Buddha of love, come to be. I am more and more convinced that Buddha won't be one person but . . . a community of love."*

"That's what I think!" I say.

"Me too," he replies.

Buddha is sangha. We teach each other through our genuine caring for one another. Koho teaches the rest of us through his humor, Cat through her steadfastness, Art through his genius at irritating the heck out of us one minute and stunning us with his unabashed kindness the next, Ron through his brilliance, Joe through his willingness to be upright in the face of monster emotions, and Anna through her refusal to give up, ever. Jack the duck teaches us by being a perfect Jack the duck. Sansae and Sanho teach us about being guardians to a community through their willingness to be there for the rest of us, whatever the need

---

* Berkeley: Parallax Press, 1997, p. 141.

is. Karen teaches the rest of us to "eat all blame" with her quick apologies.

When we're mad, sangha is our mirror. We immediately see the impact of our anger on other people. When we're sick, sangha cares for us. We squabbled over who got to take Ron to the hospital for eye surgery, for example. When Elsie died, so many people were willing to sit with her to keep her company that she had someone in her room twenty-four hours a day.

Our sangha isn't perfect. We all screw up. We fall in love, fall out of love. Without meaning to, we gossip (mostly good gossip, though). We try not to judge families and friends who don't see the wisdom of the Buddhist path. We don't proselytize—at least not on purpose. We love each other.

People come and go. This is a tough path we're committed to. Relentless even. It demands constant uprightness—seeing ourselves clearly so that we can let go of the gunk that mucks up our lives: greed for more, irritation, wanting to be fully enlightened by tomorrow noon.

It's a tough path. It mandates a habit of meditation practice. When we're lazy and find excuses not to sit, all our resistances kick in, like a computer virus that's found a way into our brains. From there, it's a slippery slope backward if we aren't careful.

Not one of us in the sangha is completely noble, although a couple of members come amazingly close. We all have faults—stuff to work out and work on.

On the other hand, *as a sangha,* we are noble. The Still Point sangha is sweet, strong, and clear. It's a community that fearlessly walks its talk. We are Detroit. We're different colors and different tastes and different views. We live hard and we play hard. We struggle to trust a political system that hasn't been kind to any of us. Some of us are gay and some of us aren't. Some of us are celibate and some of us are in relationships that range from marriage to sex once a week. We're young at twelve years old, and we're old at ninety-one. We sail through some days and we crawl through others, yearning for night.

Still Point is compassion and heartbreak and lovingkindness. We're drums and graffiti and smoggy air every day. We're joy. And if we can't solve the problems of this complicated city we call home, we can keep picking up garbage and making stupas around the city, reminding the world that *every* place is a sacred place. We can keep shining our corner. So we do.

Maitreya.

May all beings be free.

September 1, 2002

Ken Jacobson

Still Point Abbey, Detroit, Michigan